DATA STRUCTURES

Huda Noor Dean
APJ Abdul Kalam Technological University

Acknowledgements

*In the Name of Allah, the Most Gracious and Most Merciful
I begin by expressing my heartfelt gratitude to Allah for the countless
blessings that have paved the way for this endeavor.
A special acknowledgment is reserved for my parents, Noor Dean B
and Zubaida PP, whose boundless love and steadfast support have
been a constant, nurturing force in my journey.
To my beloved children, Sana Noorin and Muhammed Aman, your
ceaseless love and encouragement provided the fuel needed to embark
on and complete this venture.
To my esteemed teachers and friends, your unwavering
encouragement has been a beacon of inspiration. I am profoundly
indebted to each one of you.
This book stands as a testament to the collective support and love that
has surrounded me. I am truly blessed.*

Contents

Module 1

1.1 System Life Cycle

A system is a set of components that interacts together to achieve a goal. Systems can be considered as Large-Scale Computer Programs or information systems that contain many complex interacting parts. These programs undergo a development process called System life cycle

Different Phases of System Life Cycle

1. Requirements

   This phase analyses the problem and identifies the data (both input and output) involved in this system.

   Input: The set of data to be given to the system on which the system is processed.

   Output: The set of data expected from the system.

   A description of the problem and the input and the output which covers all cases. Following methods are usually used in this phase.

   - questionnaires
   - interviews
   - observation
   - inspection of records

2. Design

   * The designer approaches the system in terms of both representing data objects the program needs and the operations performed on them.

   * The first perspective leads to the creation of abstract data types while the second requires the specification of algorithms

     Example: Design a scheduling system for University
     Data objects: Students, courses, professors etc.
     Operations: insert, remove, search etc.

   Student object should include name, phone number, social security number etc We should be able to add a course to the list of university courses, search for the courses taught by some professor etc.

* Defining abstract data types and algorithm specifications are both language independent.

* Second perspective is ordering of processing statements. Algorithms and flowchart are two commonly used tools in this phase. For a particular problem, more than one algorithm may be created.

3. Analysis

In this phase the problem is broken down into manageable pieces and a consideration of algorithm design strategies. There are two approaches to analysis: - Bottom up and Top down Approach.

(a) Bottom-up approach is an older, unstructured strategy that places an early emphasis on coding fine points. Since the programmer does not have a master plan for the project, the resulting program frequently has many loosely connected, error ridden segments.

(b) Top-down approach is a structured approach that divides the program into manageable segments.

A given problem can have several alternate solutions. This phase also selects the most desirable algorithm depending on following performance analysis and measurements.

(a) Space complexity: Analysis of space complexity of an algorithm is the amount of memory it needs to run the algorithm to its completion.

(b) Time complexity: The time complexity of an algorithm or a program is the amount of time it needs to run to completion of the program.

4. Refinement and coding

* Data objects representation can determine the efficiency of the algorithm related to it. So, write algorithms that are independent of data objects first.

* Each statement in algorithm is further broke down into small simpler statements.

* Keep repeating the process on each statement until the statement is more specific to be implemented.

* In this stage algorithm may be represented by pseudo- code. Each abstract data type and the various functions are implemented in an appropriate programming language which is called Coding.

5. Verification

This phase consists of

(a) Developing correctness proofs for the program

  * Programs can be proven correct using proofs. (like mathematics theorem.

* Proofs are very time consuming and difficult to develop for large projects.

* Scheduling constraints prevent the development of complete sets of proofs for a larger system.

* However, selecting algorithm that have been proven correct can reduce the number of errors.

(b) Testing the program with a variety of input data.

* Testing can be done only after coding.

* Testing requires working code and set of test data.

* Test data should includes all possible scenarios.

* Good test data verifies that every piece of code runs correctly.

* For example, if our program contains a switch statement, our test data should be chosen so that we can check each case within switch statement.

(c) Removing errors.

* If done properly, the correctness of proofs and system test will indicate erroneous code.

* Removal of errors depends on the design and code.

* While debugging large undocumented program written in 'spaghetti' code, each corrected error possibly generates several new errors.

* Debugging a well-documented program that is divided into autonomous units that interact through parameters is far easier. This is especially true if each unit is tested separately and then integrated into system.

1.2 Algorithms

An algorithm is a finite set of instructions to accomplish a particular task. In addition, all algorithms must satisfy the following criteria:

- Input: Every algorithm must take zero or more number of input values from external.

- Output: Every algorithm must produce an output as result.

- Definiteness: Each instruction is clear and unambiguous.

- Finiteness: If we trace out the instructions of an algorithm, then for all cases, the algorithm terminates after a finite number of steps.

- Effectiveness: Every instruction must be basic enough to be carried out, in principle, by a person using only pencil and paper. It is not enough that each operation be definite as in (3); it also must be feasible.

We can describe algorithm in many ways:

1. We can use a natural language like English
2. Graphical Representation called flow chart, but they work well only if the algorithm is small and simple.

Example: Find the largest value in that set of numbers.

Problem Statement: Find the largest number in the given list?
Input: A list of positive integer numbers.
Output: The largest number in the given list of numbers as max.

Algorithm I

Consider the given list of numbers as 'L' (input), and the largest number as 'max' (Output).
Step 1: Define a variable 'max' and initialize with '0'.
Step 2: Compare first number (say 'x') in the list 'L' with 'max', if 'x' is larger than 'max', set 'max' to 'x'.
Step 3: Repeat step 2 for all numbers in the list 'L'.
Step 4: Display the value of 'max' as a result.

Algorithm II

Consider the given list of numbers as 'L' (input), and the largest number as 'max' (Output).
Step 1: Sort the given list in descending order.
Step 2: Assign first element in the list to 'max'
Step 3: Display the value of 'max' as a result.

Performance Analysis of an algorithm

In computer science, there may be multiple algorithms to solve a problem. When there are multiple alternative algorithms to solve a problem, we analyze them and pick the one which is best suitable for our requirements. Performance analysis helps us to select the best algorithm among the multiple algorithms designed to solve a problem. Performance analysis of an algorithm means predicting the resources which are required to an algorithm to perform its task. Two main evaluating criteria are space and time required by that particular algorithm

1.3   Complexity of an Algorithm

Performance of an algorithm is expressed as Complexity of Algorithm. The complexity of an algorithm is the function f(n) which gives the running time and/or storage space requirement of the algorithm in terms of the input data size 'n'.

   - Space required to complete the task of an algorithm is termed as **Space Complexity**.

- Time required to complete the task of an algorithm is termed as **Time Complexity** of that algorithm. Mostly, the storage space required by an algorithm is simply a multiple of the data size n. Hence, generally, complexity shall refer to the running time of the algorithm.

Best , Average and Worst case complexities The complexity of an algorithm can be measured in 3 cases:

* Best-case complexity :- It gives the minimum possible complexity f(n). Example : In the case of linear search, if the item to be searched is the first element in the list itself then it can be searched with the minimum number of iteration. It will be the best case complexity of linear search.

* Average-case complexity :- It gives the average complexity f(n). In linear search the element to be searched will be in somewhat middle.

* Worst-case complexity :-It gives maximum possible complexity f(n) of an algorithm. In the case of linear search, if the element to be searched is at the last position, then maximum number of iteration has to be performed.

1.4 Space Complexity

Analysis of space complexity of an algorithm or program is the amount of memory it needs to run to completion. The space requirement of a program depends on the following components.

* Instruction Space: It is the amount of memory used to store compiled version of instructions.

* Environmental Stack: It is the amount of memory used to store information of partially executed functions at the time of function call.

* Data Space: It is the amount of memory used to store all the variables and constants. Data space consists of:

    - Space needed for constants and simple variables in program.
    - Space needed by fixed sized structural variables, such as arrays and structures.
    - Space needed for dynamically allocated objects such as arrays and class instances.

Total Space Complexity S(P) of a program is

$$S(P) = C + Sp(I)$$

Here Sp(I) is Variable space of program P working at instance I.
C is a constant representing the fixed space requirements

```
int sum(int A[] , int n)
{
        int sum=0, i ;
        for ( i =0;i<n; i++)
        {
                sum=sum+A[ i ] ;

        }
        return sum;
}
```

Here Space needed for variable n = 1 byte, Sum = 1 byte, i = 1 byte
Array A[i] = n byte
Total Space complexity = [n+3] byte

Example 2

```
int sum (a,n)
{
        int s=0;
        for ( i =0;i<n; i++)
                for ( j=0;j<m; j++)
                        s=s+a[ i ][ j ];
        return s ;
}
```

Space needed for variable n = 1 B , m = 1 B , s = 1 B , i = 1 B, j = 1 B , Array a[i][j] = n*m Byte Total Space complexity = (n*m)+5 B

1.5   Time Complexity

Every algorithm requires some amount of computer time to execute its instruction to perform the task.

The time complexity of an algorithm is the total amount of time required by an algorithm to complete its execution.

$$T(P) = C + TP$$

Here C is compiling time and Tp is Runtime

Time Complexity can be calculated by using Two types of methods. They are:

1. Frequency Counting Method /Step Count Method.

2. Asymptotic Notation.

1.5.1 Frequency Counting Method

In this analysis, the number of times each instruction is executed is counted. The frequency of instruction executed is evaluated and finally added to get the time complexity of algorithm. The statements are assumed to have constant time complexity. The time taken by the algorithm is expressed as a function f(n), where n represents the data size. Counting the number of steps for different types of instructions

- Comments – 0 step [as step is not executed]

- Assignment statement – 1 Step

- Conditional statement – 1 Step
  In if-else statement, switch case statements, else- if ladder statements, if statement is executed only once

- Loop condition for 'n' numbers – n+1 Step
  n steps for true cases and 1 for false case

- Body of the loop – n step

- Return statement – 1 Step

It can be illustrated with the algorithm for computing the sum of 'n' numbers.

Algorithm: Sum (A[],n)	Cost/execution	Frequency	Total cost
Sum =0	c_1	1	c_1 *1
for i = 0 to n-1	c_2	n+1	c_2 * (n + 1)
Sum = Sum+ A[i]	c_3	n	c_3 * n
print sum	c_4	1	c_4 * 1

Step by step calculation of frequency count

$$\text{Total cost} = c1 * 1 + c2 * (n + 1) + c3 * n + c4 * 1$$
$$\text{Total cost} = c1 + c2 * (n + 1) + c3 * n + c4$$

Assume that all instructions have unit execution cost. ie c1,c2,c3,c4=1.
Then $\quad f(n) = 1 + (n + 1) + n + 1 = 2n + 3$

Example 1: Compute time complexity of linear search algorithm using frequency count method.

```
Algorithm: LinearSearch(A[1..n], n, key)
{
flag=0                  ----------------------------------1
```

13

```
repeat  step 3 for  i = 1 to n -----------------n+1
    if (A[i]==key)   -----------------------------n
      flag=1   ----------------------------------1
  break           ------------------------------1
if (flag == 0)               ---------------------1
  printf("Element not found")
else
printf("Element found")         -------------------1
                                          Total:2n+6
```

Example 2: Compute the frequency count of the following code fragment.

```
count := 0

for(i = 0; i < r; i++)                    n+1
{
    for(j = 0;  j < c;  j++)              n * (n+1)
    {
        if(mat[i][j] != 0)                n * n * 1
        {
            count++;                      1
        }
    }
}
```

$$f(n) = (n + 1) + n^2 + n + n^2 + 1$$
$$f(n) = 2n^2 + 2n + 2$$

1.5.2 Asymptotic Notation

The most common method of analyzing an algorithm is to express the asymptotic growth rate of algorithms with respect to its input data size. It gives the rate at which the complexity of an algorithm increases as the input data size increases. Asymptotic behavior describes a function (f (n)) with a defined limit of another function – g(n) . The function may approach this limit, getting closer and closer as the size of function's input changes, but will never reach it.
The notations used to represent the asymptotic growth rate of algorithms are called asymptotic notations.

Using asymptotic analysis, we can very well conclude the best case, average case and worst-case scenario of an algorithm Behavior of this function is usually expressed in terms of one or more standard functions.

Commonly used Asymptotic notations are:

1. Big-oh (O) Notation

2. Big- omega(Ω) Notation

3. Big-theta($\emptyset$)Notation

Let f(n) be the actual time complexity of an algorithm

$$Eg: -f(n) = 3n^2 + 2n + 4$$

Let g(n) be the asymptote by which the growth rate of f(n) is to be expressed.

1. Big-oh (O): The upper limit or the worst case growth rate

$$f(n) = O(g(n))$$

2. Big-theta(Ø): Growth in between two boundaries which is the average case

$$f(n) = Ø(g(n))$$

3. Big- omega(Ω): Asymptotic lower bound or the Best case complexity

$$f(n) = \Omega(g(n))$$

Big-oh (O) Notation

Big-O notation is the most widely used notation for Asymptotic analysis. It specifies the upper bound of the running time of an algorithm. It is defined as the condition that allows an algorithm to complete statement execution in the longest amount of time possible. The maximum time required by an algorithm or the worst-case time complexity. It returns the highest possible output value(big-O) for a given input.

Definition: If f(n) describes the running time of an algorithm, f(n) is O(g(n)) if there exist a positive constant C and n0 such that
$0 \leq f(n) \leq C * g(n)$ holds for any input size n $\geq$ n0

Then we say that f (n) is big-O of g(n). **f(n) = O(g(n))**
Example: if f(n) = 2n + 10, find the Big O notation.

```
f(n) = 2n + 10
let g(n) = n
We can write f(n) = O(n) only when the 2n + 10 <=c * g(n) hold.
          but g(n)=n, so
  2n + 10 <=c * n
  2n+ 10 - c*n =0
  (2-c)* n = -10
    let n =1 , -c = -10-2 =-12 => c = 12
```

This inequality holds for all the value n0 > 1 and c $\geq$ 12 hence 2n + 10 an be represented as O(n)

The Big-oh notation can be represented graphically as:

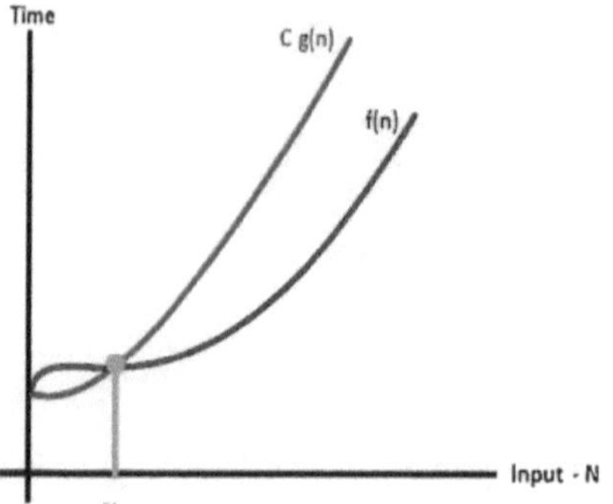

Big O: examples

$T(n)$	Complexity
$5n^3 + 200n^2 + 15$	$O(n^3)$
$3n^2 + 2^{300}$	$O(n^2)$
$5\log_2 n + 15\ln n$	$O(\log n)$
$2\log n^3$	$O(\log n)$
$4n + \log n$	$O(n)$
2^{64}	$O(1)$
$\log n^{10} + 2\sqrt{n}$	$O(\sqrt{n})$
$2^n + n^{1000}$	$O(2^n)$

Figure 1.1: Graphical representation of Big O notation and some examples

Big- omega(Ω) Notation

Omega notation represents the lower bound of the running time of an algorithm. Thus, it provides the best case, complexity of an algorithm. The execution time serves as a lower bound on the algorithm's time complexity. It is defined as the condition that allows an algorithm to complete statement execution in the shortest amount of time.

Definition: Let g and f be the function from the set of natural numbers to itself. The function f is said to be Ω(g), if there is a constant $c > 0$ and a natural number n0 such that $c * g(n) \leq$ f(n) for all $n \geq n0$

Example: f(n) = 3n + 2, find big Omega Notation

Let the complexity f(n) = 3n + 2 and g(n) = n If we want to represent f(n) as $\Omega(g(n))$ then it must satisfy $f(n) \geq Cg(n)$ for $C > 0$ and n0 >= 1

$$f(n) \geq Cg(n)$$
$$3n + 2 \geq Cn$$

Above condition is always TRUE for all values of C = 3 and $n \geq 1$ By using Big - Omega notation we can represent the time complexity as:

$$3n + 2 = \Omega(n)$$

The Big-Omega notation can be represented graphically as:

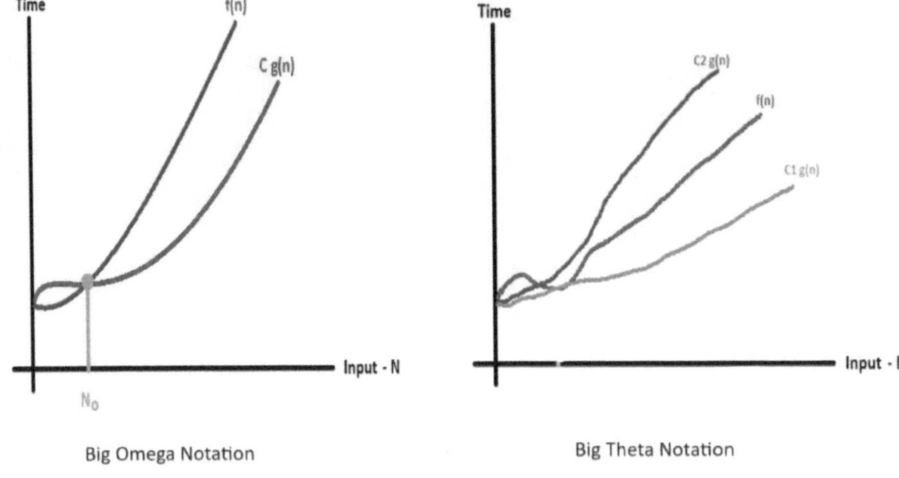

Figure 1.2: Graphical representation of Big Omega and Big Theta notations

Big-theta(Ø)Notation

Theta notation encloses the function from above and below. Since it represents the upper and the lower bound of the running time of an algorithm, it is used for analyzing the average-case complexity of an algorithm.

Let g and f be the function from the set of natural numbers to itself. The function f is said to be $\Theta(g)$, if there are constants c1,c2 > 0 and a natural number n0 such that $c1 * g(n) \leq f(n) \leq c2 * g(n)$ for all $n \geq n0$

Example: f(n) = 3n + 2, find the Big Theta notation.
Let the complexity f(n) = 3n + 2 and g(n) = n

$$f(n) = 3n + 2 g(n) = n$$

If we want to represent f(n) as $\Theta(g(n))$ then it must satisfy

```
C1*g(n) <= f(n) <= C2 * g(n) for all  values of
        C1 > 0, C2 > 0 and n0>= 1
C1*g(n) <= f(n) <= C2 * g(n)
C1 * n <= 3n + 2 <= C2 *n
```

Above condition is always TRUE for all values of C1 = 1, C2 = 4 and n ≥ 2. By using Big - Theta notation we can represent the time complexity as follows...
$$3n + 2 = \Theta(n)$$

Example: $f(n) = 2n^2 + 3n + 4$

$$=> 2n^2 + 3n + 4 \leq 2n^2 + 3n^2 + 4n^2$$

$$2n^2 + 3n + 4 \leq 9n^2, n \geq 1$$
$$c = 9, g(n) = n^2$$
$$f(n) = O(g(n))$$
$$= O(n^2)$$
$$=> 2n^2 + 3n + 4 \leq 1n^2$$
$$\Omega(n^2)$$
$$=> 1n^2 \leq 2n^2 + 3n + 4 \leq 9n^2$$
$$\Theta(n^2)$$

Time complexity of binary search

In Binary search algorithm, the target key is examined in a sorted sequence and this algorithm starts searching with the middle item of the sorted sequence.

- If the middle item is the target value, then the search item is found and it returns True.

- If the target item $<$ middle item, then search for the target value in the first half of the list.

- If the target item $>$ middle item, then search for the target value in the second half of the list.

In Binary Search, each comparison eliminates about half of the items from the list. Consider a list with n items, then about n/2 items will be eliminated after first comparison. After second comparison, n/4 items of the list will be eliminated. If this process is repeated for several times, then there will be just one item left in the list.

The number of comparisons required to reach to this point is n/2i = 1. If we solve for i, then it gives us i = log2 n. The maximum number of comparisons is logarithmic in nature, hence the time complexity of binary search is O(log n).

Module 2

Data structures are a specific way of organizing data in a specialized format on a computer so that the information can be organized, processed, stored, and retrieved quickly and effectively. They are a means of handling information, rendering the data for easy use. It represents a logical relationship between individual elements of data. It is defined as a mathematical model of particular organization of data items. It is also called as the building block of a program.

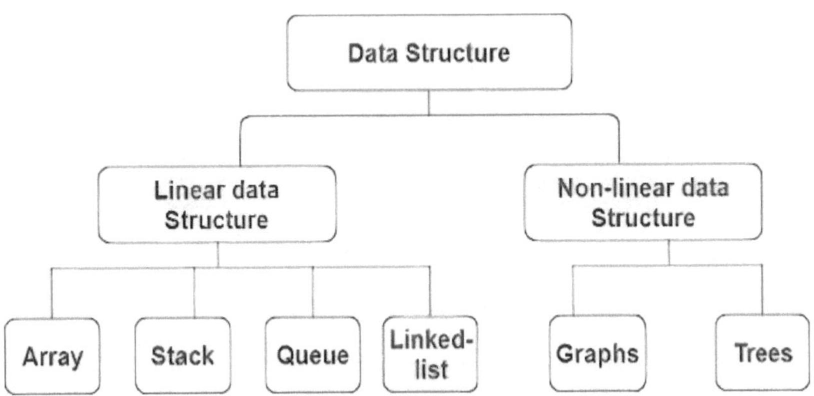

Figure 2.1: Classification of classic data structures

1. Linear data structure: In a linear data structure, data elements are arranged in a sequential or linear fashion. Each element is attached with its next and previous element. There is only has one level data, so traversals can be done in a single run. Since computer memory is linearly arranged, linear data structures are simple to implement. Linear data structure examples are array, linked list, stack, queue, etc.

2. Nonlinear data structure : Data structures where data element are not arranged in a linear or sequential fashion is referred as nonlinear data structure. As a nonlinear structure has more than one level of data it is impossible to traverse in one run. Linear data structures are easy to implement compared to Nonlinear data structures. But Nonlinear make use of computer memory

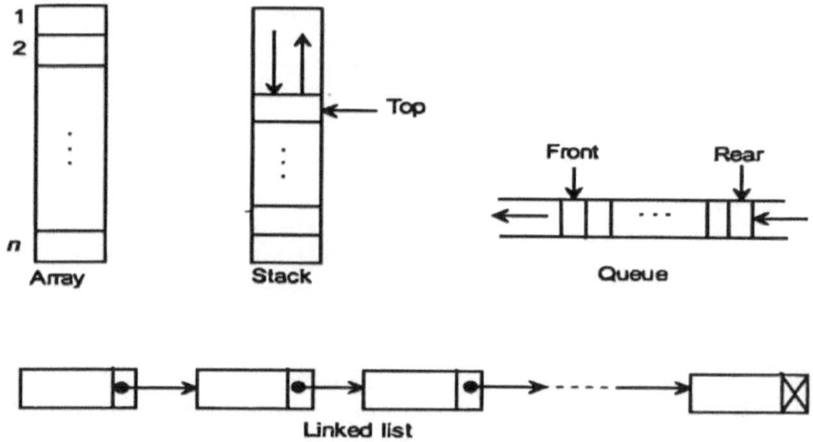

Figure 2.2: Linear Data Structures

effectively than linear structure. Examples of this are graphs and trees.

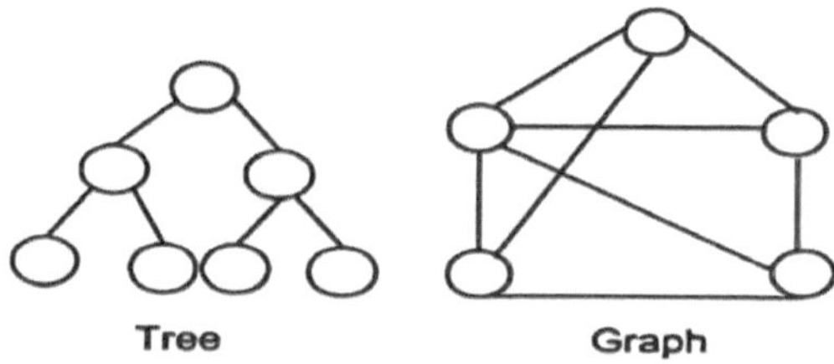

Figure 2.3: Non Linear Data Structures

2.1 Polynomial representation using arrays

Polynomials and Sparse Matrix are two important applications of arrays and linked lists. A polynomial is composed of different terms where each of them holds a coefficient and an exponent. A polynomial is a sum of terms where each term has the form ax^e , where x is the variable, a is the coefficient and e is the exponent. A polynomial p(x) is the expression in variable x which is in the form $a_n x^n + a_{n-1} x^{n-1} + \cdots + a_1 x + a_0$ where $a_n, a_{n-1}, \cdots, a_1, a_0$ falls in the category of real numbers and 'n' is non negative integer, which is called the degree of polynomial.

An essential characteristic of the polynomial is that each term in the polynomial expression consists of two parts: one is the coefficient and other is the exponent.

Example:
$10x^2 + 26x$, here 10 and 26 are coefficients and 2, 1 is its exponential value.

The sign of each coefficient and exponent is stored within the coefficient and the exponent itself
Example: $-40x^6 + 6x^3$, here -40 and 6 are coefficients and 6, 3 is its exponential value.

The storage allocation for each term in the polynomial must be done in ascending and descending order of their exponent Polynomial can be represented in the various ways. These are:
1.By the use of arrays
2. By the use of Linked List

Representation using Arrays

Array representation assumes that the exponents of the given expression are arranged from 0 to the highest value (degree), which is represented by the subscript of the array beginning with 0. The coefficients of the respective exponent are placed at an appropriate index in the array.

Example: $4x^6 - 2x + 5$,
The array representation for the above polynomial expression is given below:

0	1	2	3	4	5	6	——— Exponent
5	-2	0	0	0	0	4	——— Coefficient

Figure 2.4: Array Representation of Polynomials

That is

- the coefficient 5 is in slot 0 of the array (representing $5x^0$)

- the coefficient -2 is in slot 1 of the array (representing $-2x^1$)

- the coefficient 4 is in slot 6 of the array (representing $4x^6$)

The disadvantage here is, lots of space is wasted for storing zero coefficients. Another efficient way is to store polynomial is using array of structures.

```
struct Poly
{
  int coeff;
  int exp;

}P[20];
```

This array of structures can be to store a polynomial of 20 terms.

Example: $3x^5 + 2x^4 + 5x^2 + 2x + 7$, The array representation for the above polynomial expression is given below:

3	2	5	2	7	Coefficient
5	4	2	1	0	Exponent

Figure 2.5: Array of structure Representation of Polynomials

Example: Represent $P(x,y) = 10x^7y^7 + 5x^6y^5 + 4x^4y^2 + 8x^2 + 25$ using array of structures

```
struct Poly
{
  int coeff;
  int xexp;
  int yexp;
}P[20];
```

10	5	4	8	25	Coefficient
7	6	4	2	0	X-Exponent
7	5	2	0	0	Y-Exponent

Figure 2.6: Array of structure Representation of Polynomial in two variables

Algorithm : PolyArrayAdd
Input : Two polynomials A and B of degree m and n respectively.
Output : Polynomial C with higher degree of A or B.
Data structure : Array representation of polynomials A, B, C.

```
Step1: Create an array C [ ] of size equal to maximum of 'm' and 'n'
Step 2: if ( m >  n )
Step 3:         Copy A [ ] to C [ ].
Step 4:         Traverse array B[] and for every element of B[i]
Step 5:            C [i] = C [i] + B[i]
                [End loop]
Step 6: else
Step 7:         Copy B [ ] to C [ ].
Step 8:         Traverse array A[] and for every element of A[i]
Step 9:            C [i] = C [i] + A [i]
                [End loop]
           [End If]
Step 10: Return
```

2.2 Sparse Matrix using Array

A matrix is a two-dimensional data object made of 'm' rows and 'n' columns, therefore having total m x n values. If most of the elements of the matrix have 0 values, then it is called a **sparse matrix.**Sparse matrix is a matrix which contains very few non-zero elements.

Consider a matrix of size **100 x 100** containing only **10 non-zero** elements. In this matrix, **only 10 spaces are filled** with non-zero values and remaining spaces of the matrix are filled with zero. Totally we all allocate 100 X 100 X 2 = 20000 bytes of space to store this integer matrix. To access these 10 non-zero elements, we have to make scanning for 10000 times.

* Storage: Lesser memory is used to store only those non-zero elements.

* Computing time: Computing time can be saved by traversing only non-zero elements.

A sparse matrix can be stores as triples- (Row, Column, value) instead of storing zeroes. Sparse Matrix Representations can be done in many ways following are two common representations:

1. By the use of arrays

2. By the use of Linked List

Representation using Arrays

2D array is used to represent a sparse matrix in which there are three rows :

- Row: Index of row of the non-zero element located.

- Column: Index of column of the non-zero element located.

- Value: Value of the non-zero element located at A[i][j]

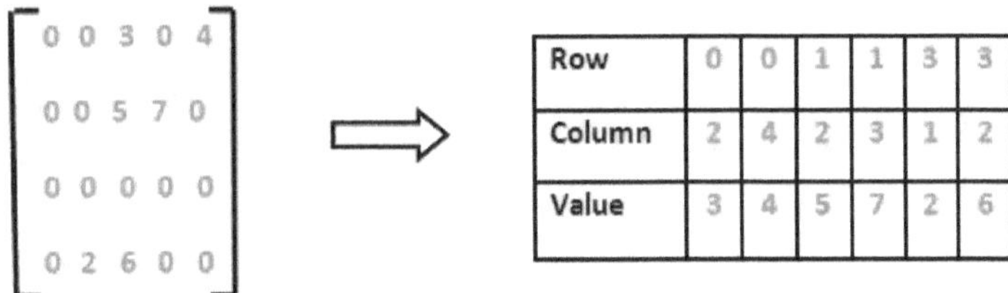

Figure 2.7: Sparse Matrix Representation using Arrays

Time Complexity : O(NM), where N is the number of rows in the sparse matrix, and M is the number of columns in the sparse matrix.

Auxiliary Space : O(NM), where N is the number of rows in the sparse matrix, and M is the number of columns in the sparse matrix.

Algorithm : CreateSparse
Input : A matrix of size N X N .
Output : Sparse Matrix with k non-zero elements.
Data structure : Array representation of Sparse Matrix SM.

```
Step 1: Read Matrix A[N][N] with R rows and C Columns
Step 2: Set k=0
Step 3: Repeat Steps 4  for i=0 to R-1
Step 4:    Repeat Steps  5 for j=0 to C-1
Step 5:        if ( A[i][j] != 0)
Step 6:            Set SM[0][k]=i
Step 7:            Set SM[1][k]=j
Step 8:            Set SM[2][k]=A[i][j]
Step 9:            k=k+1
               [End if]
            [End while]
         [End while]
Step 10: Return
```

Representation Using Linked Lists In linked list, each node has four fields. These four fields are defined as:

- Row: Index of row of the non-zero element located.

- Column: Index of column of the non-zero element located.

- Value: Value of the non-zero element located at $A[i][j]$

- Next node: Address of the next node

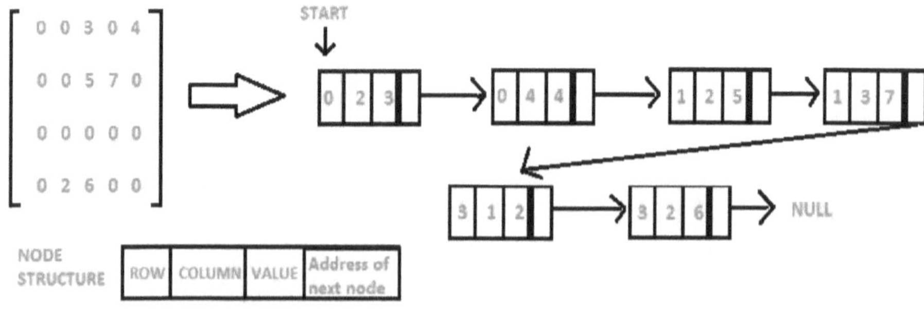

Figure 2.8: Sparse Matrix Representation using Arrays

2.3 Stack

It is a linear data structure in which elements are placed one above another. A **Stack** is an ordered collection of homogeneous data elements where the insertion and deletion operations take place only at one end called Top of the stack. In stack elements are arranged in Last-In-First-Out manner (LIFO). So, it is also called LIFO data structure. Anything added to the stack goes on the "top" of the stack. Anything removed from the stack is taken from the "top" of the stack. Things are removed in the reverse order from that in which they were inserted.

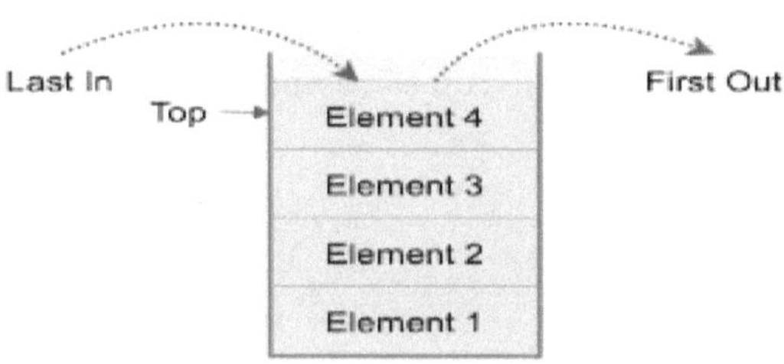

Figure 2.9: Stack as LIFO data structure

Array representation of Stack Stack can be represented using a linear array. There is a pointer called TOP to indicate the top of the stack.

Properties of Stack

- An element in the stack is termed as an ITEM.

- Initially TOP is set to -1, to indicate that the stack is empty.

- The maximum no. of elements that a stack can accommodate is termed as MAX_SIZE.

- If stack is full Top = MAX_SIZE - 1

  Overflow : If we try to insert a new element in the stack top which is already full, then the situation is called stack overflow.

  Underflow : If we try to remove an element from an empty stack, the situation is called stack underflow.

Operations of Stack Basic operations of stack are:

1. PUSH : Insert an element at the top of stack.

2. POP : Delete an element from the top of stack.

3. PEEK : Display the element on top of stack.

Push Operation

The process of putting a new data element onto stack is known as Push Operation.
Push operation involves a series of steps -
Step 1 - Checks if the stack is full.
Step 2 - If the stack if full, produces an overflow error and exit.
Step 3 - If the stack is not full, increments top to point next empty space.
Step 4 - Adds data element to the stack location, where top is pointing.
Step 5 - Returns success.
Algorithm : PUSH(ITEM)
Input : ITEM is inserted to stack.
Output : Stack with ITEM inserted at position Top.
Data structure : An array A with Top as the pointer.

```
1.    if Top >= MAX_SIZE - 1
2.         print "OVERFLOW"
3.    else
4.         Set Top=Top+1
5.         Set A[Top]=ITEM
      [end if]
6. Return
```

Pop Operation

The process of removing a data element from the stack is known as Pop Operation.
Pop operation involves a series of steps -
Step 1 - Checks if the stack is empty.
Step 2 - if the stack is empty, produces an error and exit.
Step 3 - if the stack is not empty, accesses the data element at which **top** is pointing.
Step 4 - Decreases the value of top by 1.
Step 5 - Returns success.

Algorithm : POP()
Input : ITEM is removed from stack.
Output : Stack with ITEM removed from position Top if stack not empty.
Data structure : An array A with Top as the pointer.

```
1.    if Top < 1
2.         print "UNDERFLOW"
3.    else
4.         Set ITEM=A[Top]
5.         Set Top=Top-1
      [end if]
6. Return
```

Peek Operation

This operation shows the status of Stack, if empty or full. It also returns the Top element from the stack, if not empty. This is known as Peek Operation.

Peek operation involves a series of steps -
Step 1 - Checks if the stack is empty.
Step 2 - if the stack is empty, produces an error and exit.
Step 3 - if the stack is full, produces an error and Step 4 - if the stack is not empty, accesses the data element at which **top** is pointing.
Step 5 - Returns success.

Algorithm : PEEK()
Input : Status of Stack is given.
Output : Message if stack is full or empty and Top element is returned if stack not empty.
Data structure : An array A with Top as the pointer.

```
1.    if Top < 1
2.        print "Stack is empty"
3.    else
4.            if Top >= MAX_SIZE - 1
5.                print "Stack full"
6.        Set ITEM=A[Top]
7.        Print "ITEM"
     [End if]
7. Return
```

Applications of stack

1. Reversing an array

2. Infix to prefix, infix to postfix conversion

3. Evaluation of postfix expressions

4. Tree Traversal

2.4 Queue

A queue is an ordered collection of homogeneous data elements. In which insertion is done at one end called REAR and deletion is done at another end called FRONT. In queue elements are arranged in First-In-First-Out manner (FIFO). First inserted element is removed first.

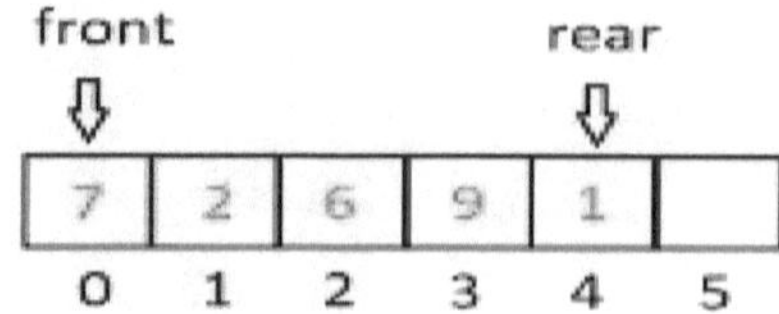

Figure 2.10: Queue as FIFO data structure

Array representation of Queue Queue can be represented using a linear array. There are two pointers called FRONT and REAR, which represents two ends of the Queue. Insertion into a Queue takes place at the REAR and Deletion in a Queue takes place from the front of the Queue

Properties of Queue

- Initial case rear = -1 and front = -1, MAX_SIZE is the size of the queue.

- If rear = front then queue contains only a single element

- Queue full : rear = n-1 and front =0

- Whenever an element is deleted from the queue, the value of FRONT is increased by 1. i.e. FRONT=FRONT+1

- Whenever an element is added to the queue, the REAR is incremented by 1 as, REAR=REAR+1

  Overflow : If we try to insert a new element to a queue which is already full, then the situation is called Queue overflow.

  Underflow : If we try to remove an element from an empty Queue, the situation is called Queue underflow.

Operations of Queue

Basic operations of stack are:

1. ENQUEUE : Insert an element at the Rear of Queue.
2. DEQUEUE : Delete an element from the Front of Queue.

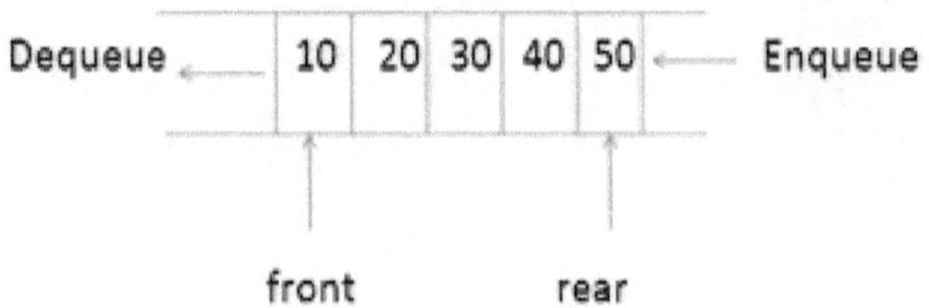

Figure 2.11: Queue with operations

Enqueue Operation

The process of putting a new data element into a Queue is known as Enqueue Operation.

Enqueue operation involves a series of steps -
Step 1 - Checks if the Queue is full.
Step 2 - If the Queue if full, produces an overflow error and exit.
Step 3 - If the Queue is not full, increments Rear to point next empty space.
Step 4 - Adds data element to the Queue location, where Rear is pointing.
Step 5 - Returns success.

Algorithm : Enqueue(ITEM)
Input : ITEM is inserted to Queue.
Output : Queue with ITEM inserted at rear.
Data structure : An array Q with Front and Rear as two pointers.

```
1.    if Rear = MAX_SIZE - 1            //Queue is full
2.        print "OVERFLOW"
3.    else
4.        if (rear=-1) and (Front=-1)      //Queue is empty
5.         Front=0
      [end if]
6.      Rear=Rear+1
7.      Q[Rear]=ITEM              //Insert ITEM at Rear
      [end if]
8. Return
```

Dequeue Operation

The process of removing a data element from the Queue is known as Dequeue Operation.

Dequeue operation involves a series of steps -
Step 1 - Checks if the Queue is empty.
Step 2 - if the Queue is empty, produces an Underflow error and exit.
Step 3 - if the Queue is not empty, accesses the data element at which **Front** is pointing.
Step 4 - Increases the value of Front by 1.
Step 5 - Returns success.

Algorithm : DEQUEUE()
Input : ITEM is removed from Queue.
Output : Queue with ITEM removed from position Front if Queue not empty.
Data structure : An array Q with Front and Rear as two pointers.

```
1.    if Front = -1
2.        print "QUEUE is empty"
3.    else
4.        Set ITEM=Q[Front]
5.        if(Front=Rear)              // only one element in Queue
6.              Front=-1, Rear =-1        //Queue becomes empty
7.        else
8.              Front=Front+1
          [end if]
      [end if]
9. Return
```

Let us trace Enqueue and Dequeue on a queue with size as 10. Suppose the current state is Front =8 and Rear=9 . Let ten operations be executed as follows:

    1. DEQUEUE   2. ENQUEUE   3. ENQUEUE   4. DEQUEUE
    5. DEQUEUE   6. DEQUEUE   7. ENQUEUE   8. ENQUEUE
    9. DEQUEUE   10. DEQUEUE

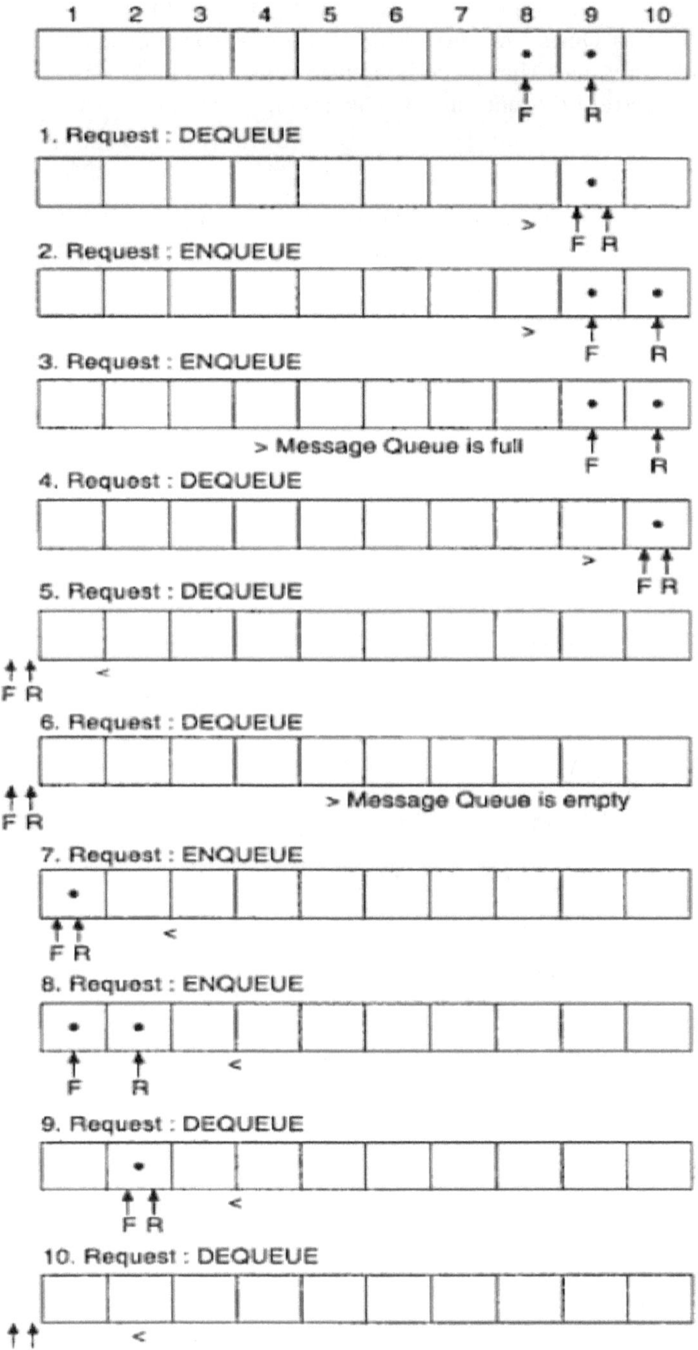

Figure 2.12: Queue with operations

From this example, we can see that for the request (3) for Enqueue, gives a wrong message as Queue full, even though there is space in Queue. Insertion is then possible only once the queue is empty, which is simple wastage of storage. Following Requests show that, once Queue is empty we can reuse the Queue again.

Peek Operation

This operation shows the status of Queue, if empty or full. It also returns the Front element from the Queue, if not empty. This is known as Peek Operation.

Peek operation involves a series of steps -
Step 1 - Checks if the Queue is empty.
Step 2 - if the Queue is empty, produces an msg as Queue empty and exit.
Step 3 - if the Queue is full, produces msg as Queue full.
Step 4 - if the stack is not empty, accesses the data element at which **front** is pointing.
Step 5 - Returns success.

Algorithm : PEEK()
Input : Status of Queue is given.
*Output :*Message if Queue is full or empty and Front element is returned if Q not empty.
Data structure : An array Q with Front and Rear as two pointers.

```
1.   if Rear < 0
2.       print "Queue  is empty"
3.   else
4.            if Rear= MAX_SIZE - 1
5.              print "Queue is full"
6.       Set ITEM=A[Front]
7.       Print "ITEM"
     [End if]
7. Return ITEM
```

Type of Queues

1. Circular Queue

2. Priority Queue

3. Double ended Queue

2.5   Circular Queue

To utilize space properly, circular queue is derived. In this queue the elements are inserted in circular manner. So that no space is wasted at all. Physically, a circular Queue is the same as an ordinary array say Q[0,1,....N-1], where N is the size of the Queue. But logically it implies that Q[0] comes after Q[N-1].

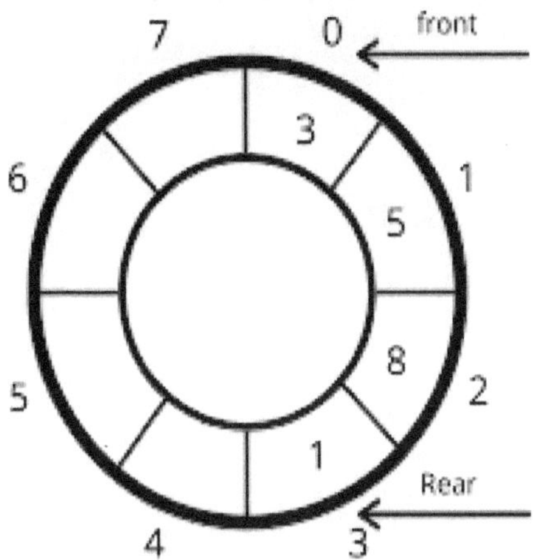

Figure 2.13: Circular Queue of size 8

The figure shows a circular Queue of Size 8 , numbered from 0 to 7. Q[0] follows Q[7]. Both the pointers Front and Rear move in clockwise direction. This is done with the help of MOD operation.

Circular queue empty: FRONT= -1 and REAR= -1
Circular queue full: (REAR + 1) MOD N = FRONT.

It is a modification of simple queue in which the Rear pointer is set to the initial location 0, whenever it reaches the location N − 1. Same as Front is set to 0 after removing an element at N-1.

Enqueue Operation

The process of putting a new data element into a Circular Queue is known as Enqueue Operation.

Enqueue operation involves a series of steps -
Step 1 - Checks if the Circular Queue is full.
Step 2 - If the Circular Queue if full, produces an overflow error and exit.
Step 3 - If the Circular Queue is not full, increments Rear to point next empty space. If Rear= N-1, then set Rear =0
Step 4 - Adds data element to the Circular Queue location, where Rear is pointing.
Step 5 - Returns success.

Algorithm : Enqueue(ITEM)

Input : ITEM is inserted to Circular Queue.

Output : Circular Queue with ITEM inserted at rear if not full.

Data structure : An array CQ with Front and Rear as two pointers of size N.

```
1.    if ( Front= ( Rear +1 )  MOD N )          //Queue is full
2.        print "OVERFLOW"
3.    else
4.        if (Rear=-1) and (Front=-1)        //Queue is empty
5.         Front=0
    [end if]
6.        Rear= (Rear+1) MOD N
7.        CQ[Rear]=ITEM              //Insert ITEM at Rear
    [end if]
8. Return
```

Dequeue Operation

The process of removing a data element from the Circular Queue is known as Dequeue Operation.

Dequeue operation involves a series of steps -

Step 1 - Checks if the Circular Queue is empty.

Step 2 - if the Circular Queue is empty, produces an underflow error and exit.

Step 3 - if the Circular Queue is not empty, accesses the data element at which **Front** is pointing.

Step 4 - Increases the value of Front by 1. If Front= N-1, then set Front =0

Step 5 - Returns success.

Algorithm : DEQUEUE()

Input : ITEM is removed from Circular Queue.

Output : Circular Queue with ITEM removed from Front if Queue not empty.

Data structure : An array CQ with Front and Rear as two pointers of size N.

```
1.    if Front = -1
2.        print "QUEUE is empty"
3.    else
4.        Set ITEM=CQ[Front]
5.        if(Front=Rear)              // only one element in Queue
6.              Front=-1, Rear =-1      //Queue becomes empty
7.        else
8.              Front=(Front+1)MOD N
        [end if]
    [end if]
9. Return ITEM
```

2.6 Priority Queue

A priority queue is a type of queue that arranges elements based on their priority values. An element is added to the queue, in a position based on its priority value. For example, if you add an element with a high priority value to a priority queue, it may be inserted near the front of the queue, while an element with a low priority value may be inserted near the back. Elements with higher priority values are typically retrieved before elements with lower priority values.

Properties of Priority Queue

- In a priority queue, each element has a priority value associated with it.

- An element with high priority is dequeued before an element with low priority.

- If two elements have the same priority, they are served according to their order in the queue.

- When you add an element to the queue, it is inserted in a position based on its priority value.

There are several ways to implement a priority queue, including using an array, linked list, heap, or binary search tree. Each method has its own advantages and disadvantages, and the best choice will depend on the specific needs of your application. The binary heap is the most efficient method for implementing the priority queue.

Types of Priority Queue

1. Ascending order priority queue:
   The element with the lowest value can be assigned the highest priority and the element with the highest value is assigned the lowest priority. For example, if five numbers come to be inserted in the priority queue that are 10, 6, 2, 1, 7. Firstly, they are arranged in ascending order. The new list is as follows: 2,6,7,10,11. In this list, 2 is the smallest number. Hence, the ascending order priority queue treats number 2 as the highest priority and 11 as the lowest priority.

Figure 2.14: Ascending order priority queue

2. Descending order priority queue:

The element with the highest value is assigned the highest priority and the
element with the lowest value is assigned the lowest priority. For example, if
five numbers come to be inserted in the priority queue that are 10, 6, 8, 9, 7.
First arrange these numbers in descending order. The new list is as follows:
10, 9,8,7,6. In this list, 10 is the highest number. Hence, the descending
order priority queue treats number 10 as the highest priority and 6 has the
lowest priority.

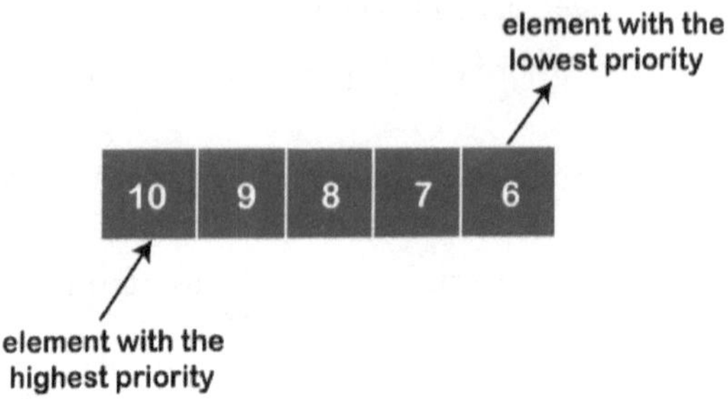

Figure 2.15: Descending order priority queue

Operations in Priority queue using arrays

Whenever an element is inserted into queue, priority queue inserts the item according to its order. Here we're assuming that data with high value has low priority.

- EnQueue: EnQueue operation inserts an item into the queue. The item can
  be inserted depending either on its priority (ordered array) or at the end of
  Queue (unordered Array)

- DeQueue: DeQueue operation removes the item with the highest priority
  from the queue.

- Peek: Peek operation reads the item with the highest priority.

Priority Queue can be implemented in two ways:

- Using ordered Array: In ordered array insertion or enqueue operation takes
  O(n) time complexity because it enters elements in sorted order in queue.
  And deletion takes O(1) time complexity.

- Using unordered Array: In unordered array deletion takes O(n) time complexity because it search for the element in Queue for the deletion and enqueue takes O(1) time complexity.

1. **Using an ordered array:**

The item is inserted in such a way that the array remains ordered i.e. the largest item is always in the end. The insertion operation is illustrated in figure. The item with priority 7 is inserted between the items with priorities 6 and 8. Since we must scan through the queue in order to find the appropriate position to insert the new item, the worst-case complexity of this operation is O(n).

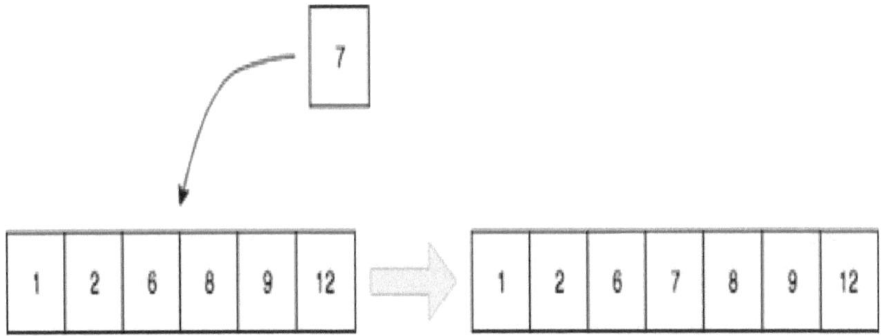

Figure 2.16: Insertion operation in an ordered array

For deletion, we remove the item with highest priority. Since the item with the highest priority is always in the first position, the dequeue and peek operation takes a constant time O(1).

2. **Using an unordered array:**

We can insert it at the end of the queue, then the array becomes unordered. The complexity of this operation is O(1). Since the queue is not ordered, we need to search through the queue for the item with maximum priority. Once we remove this item, we need to shift all the items after it one step to the left. The dequeue operation is illustrated in figure.

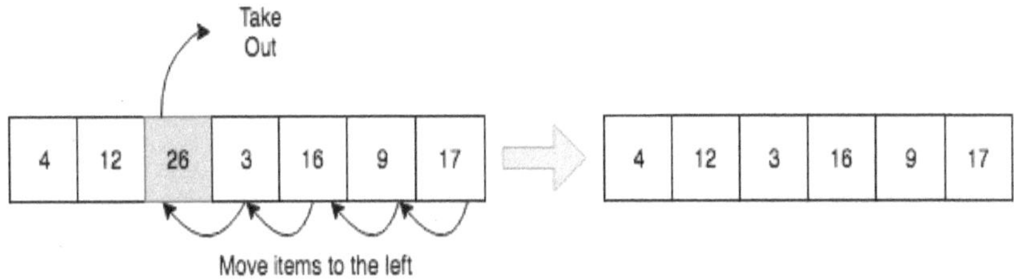

Figure 2.17: Dequeue operation in an unordered array

It is obvious that the complexity of dequeue and peek operation is O(n). Since it requires searching the whole array for the highest priority element.

Here, we illustrate algorithm for enqueue and Dequeue operation in an ordered Array. For ease of understanding Linear Queue has been used. It can be implemented using Circular queue also.

Algorithm : Enqueue(ITEM)

Input :   ITEM is inserted to Priority Queue.
Output :   Priority Queue with ITEM inserted at position if not full to get a sorted array.
Data structure : An array PQ with Front and Rear as two pointers of size N.

```
1.    if ( Rear = N-1 )          //Queue is full
2.        print "OVERFLOW"
3.    else
4.        if (Rear=-1) and (Front=-1)        //Queue is empty
5.            Front=0 , Rear=0
6.            PQ[Rear]=ITEM
7.       else
8.           i=REAR+1
9.          Repeat steps 10,11 while(item<QUEUE[i-1] and i>0)
10              PQ[i]=PQ[i-1]
11.             SET i=i-1
               [End while]
12.          PQ[i]=item;
           [End if]
13.   REAR=REAR+1
      [end if]
14. Return
```

Algorithm : DEQUEUE()

Input :   ITEM is removed from Priority Queue.
Output :   Priority Queue with ITEM removed from position Front if Queue not empty.
Data structure : An array PQ with Front and Rear as two pointers of size N.

```
1.    if Front = -1
2.        print "QUEUE is empty"
3.    else
4.        Set ITEM=Q[Front]
5.        if(Front=Rear)              // only one element in Queue
```

```
6.                   Front=-1, Rear =-1        //Queue becomes empty
7.          else
8.                  Front=Front+1
            [end if]
        [end if]
9. Return ITEM
```

Applications of Priority queue

1. It is used in the Dijkstra's shortest path algorithm and in prim's algorithm.

2. It is used in heap sort.

3. It is also used in operating system like priority scheduling, load balancing and interrupt handling.

2.7 Double ended Queue - Deque

The deque stands for Double Ended Queue. Deque is a linear data structure where the insertion and deletion operations are performed from both ends. It does not follow the FIFO rule. Deque is a generalized version of the queue.

Representation of deque

There are two types of deque –

1. Input restricted queue.

2. Output restricted queue.

Input restricted queue

In input restricted queue, insertion operation can be performed at only one end, while deletion can be performed from both ends.

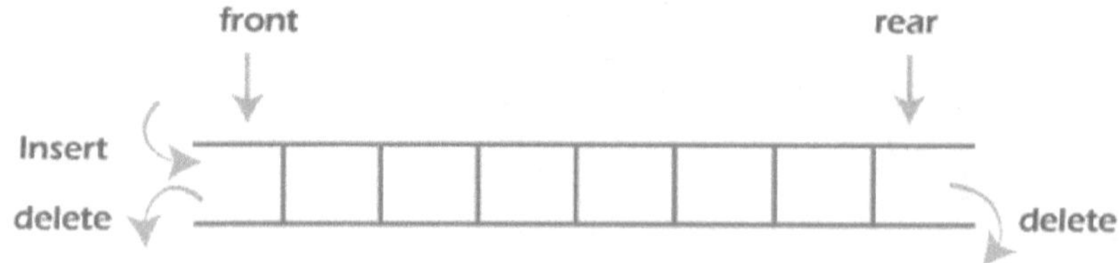

input restricted double ended queue

Input restricted queue

In output restricted queue, deletion operation can be performed at only one end, while insertion can be performed from both ends.

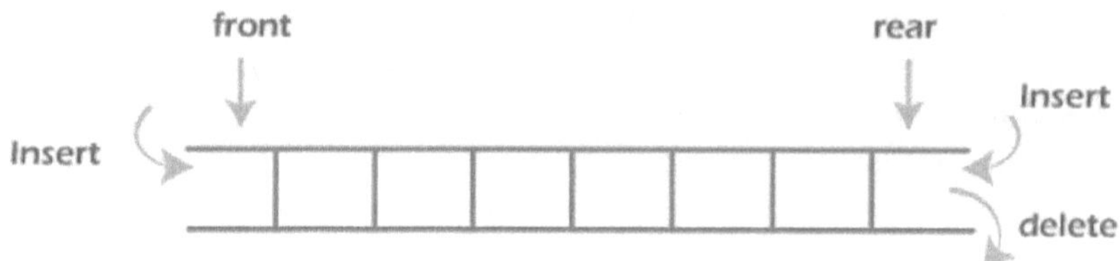

Output restricted double ended queue

Circular array implementation deque

For implementing deque, we need to keep track of two indices, front and rear. We enqueue(push) an item at the rear or the front end of deque and dequeue(pop) an item from both rear and front end.

Insert Elements at Front

First, we check if the queue is full. If it's not full we insert an element at front end by following the given conditions:

If the queue is empty then initialize front and rear to 0. Both will point to the first element.

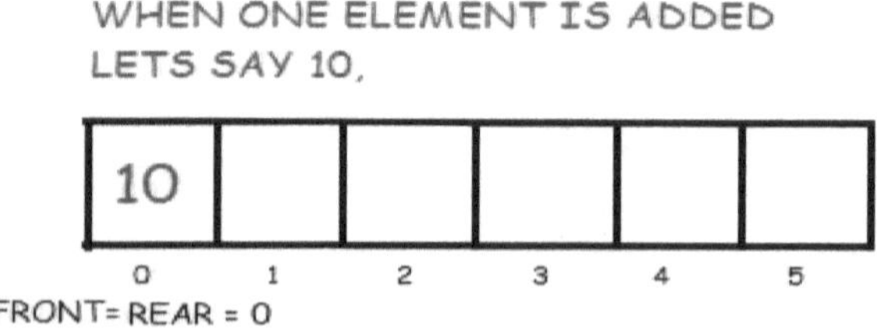

Else we decrement Front and insert the element (Front=Front-1). Since we are using circular array, we have to keep in mind that if front is equal to 0 then instead of decreasing it by 1 we make it equal to SIZE-1.

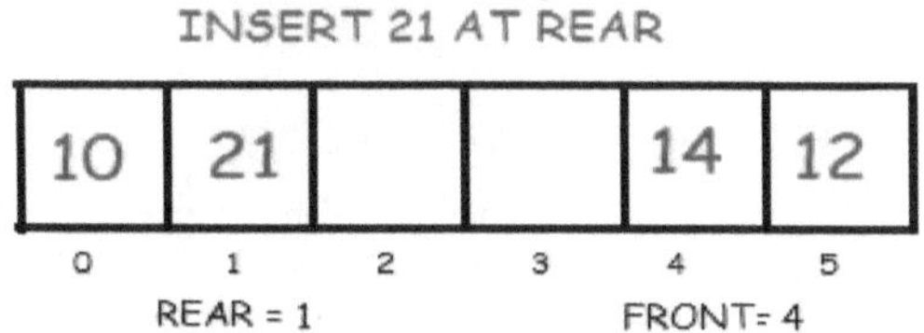

Insert Elements at back

Again, we check if the queue is full. If it's not full we insert an element at back by following the given conditions:

If the queue is empty then initialize front and rear to 0. Both will point to the first element.

Else we increment rear and insert the element. Since we are using circular array, we have to keep in mind that if rear is equal to SIZE-1 then instead of increasing it by 1 we make it equal to 0.

Delete Element from Front

In order to do this, we first check if the queue is empty. If it's not, then delete the front element by following the given conditions:

If only one element is present, we once again make front and rear equal to -1.

Else we increment front. But we have to keep in mind that if front is equal to SIZE-1 then instead of increasing it by 1 we make it equal to 0.

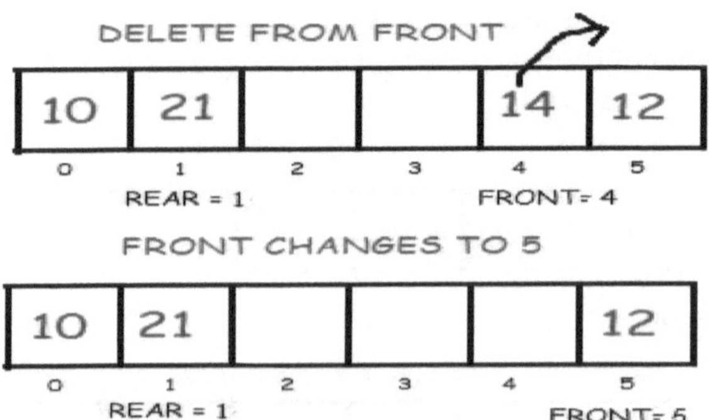

Delete Element from back

In order to do this, we again first check if the queue is empty. If it's not then we delete the last element by following the given conditions:

If only one element is present, we make front and rear equal to -1.

Else we decrement rear. But we have to keep in mind that if rear is equal to 0 then instead of decreasing it by 1 we make it equal to SIZE-1.

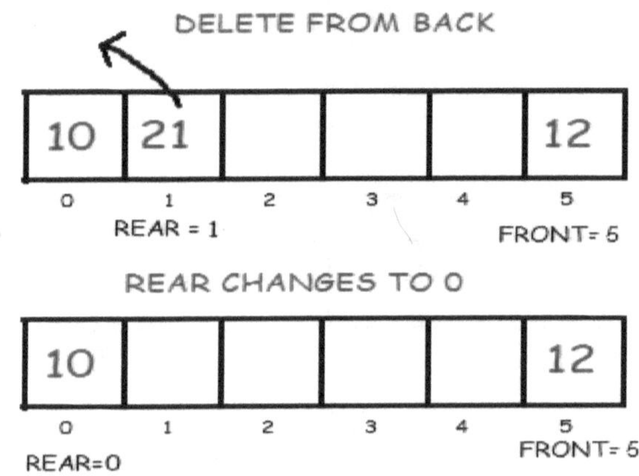

Operations performed on Deque

The operations of insertion and deletion can be summarized as follows:

- Insertion at front (Injection)   Insertion at rear (Enqueue)
- Deletion from front (Dequeue)   Deletion from rear (Ejection)

Algorithm : Inject(ITEM)

Input :   ITEM is inserted to Double Ended Queue.
Output :   Double Ended Queue with ITEM inserted at Front if not full.
Data structure : An array DQ with Front and Rear as two pointers of size N.

```
1.    if ( Front= ( Rear +1 )  MOD N )        //Queue is full
2.       print "OVERFLOW"
```

```
3.    else
4.        if (Rear=-1) and (Front=-1)        //Queue is empty
5.          Front=0, Rear=0
      [end if]
6.       Front=(Front-1)MOD N
7.       DQ[Front]=ITEM                //Insert ITEM at Front
    [end if]
8. Return
```

Algorithm : Enqueue(ITEM)

Input : ITEM is inserted to Double Ended Queue.

Output : Double Ended Queue with ITEM inserted at rear if not full.

Data structure : An array DQ with Front and Rear as two pointers of size N.

```
1.    if ( Front= ( Rear +1 )  MOD N )        //Queue is full
2.        print "OVERFLOW"
3.    else
4.        if (Rear=-1) and (Front=-1)        //Queue is empty
5.          Front=0 ,Rear=0
      [end if]
6.        Rear= (Rear+1) MOD N
7.        DQ[Rear]=ITEM                //Insert ITEM at Rear
    [end if]
8. Return
```

Algorithm : Dequeue()

Input : ITEM is removed from Double Ended Queue.

Output : Double Ended Queue with ITEM removed from position Front if Queue not empty.

Data structure : An array DQ with Front and Rear as two pointers of size N.

```
1.    if Front = -1
2.        print "QUEUE is empty"
3.    else
4.        Set ITEM=DQ[Front]
5.        if(Front=Rear)                // only one element in Queue
6.              Front=-1, Rear =-1        //Queue becomes empty
7.        else
8.              Front=(Front+1)MOD N
          [end if]
      [end if]
9. Return ITEM
```

Algorithm : Eject()

Input : ITEM is removed from Double Ended Queue.

Output : Double Ended Queue with ITEM removed from position Rear if Queue not empty.

Data structure : An array DQ with Front and Rear as two pointers of size N.

```
1.    if Front = -1
2.        print "QUEUE is empty"
3.    else
4.        Set ITEM=DQ[Front]
5.        if(Front=Rear)              // only one element in Queue
6.              Front=-1, Rear =-1        //Queue becomes empty
7.        else
8.              Rear=(Rear-1)MOD N
          [end if]
       [end if]
9. Return ITEM
```

2.8 Evaluation of expressions

An arithmetic expression can contain parentheses and binary operations (+, -, *, and /) as well. Arithmetic Expressions can be written in one of three forms:

- Infix Notation: Operators are written between the operands e.g. $3 + 4$.

- Prefix Notation: Operators are written before the operands, e.g. $+\ 3\ 4$

- Postfix Notation: Operators are written after operands. e.g. $3\ 4\ +$

Infix Expressions are harder for computers to evaluate because of the additional work needed to decide precedence. Infix notation is how expressions are written and recognized by humans and, generally, input to programs. Given that they are harder to evaluate, they are generally converted to one of the two remaining forms, either postfix or prefix expression before evaluation. Here we convert an infix to postfix conversion. It consists of two steps.

1. Convert an expression into its postfix notation.

2. Evaluate the expression in postfix notation.

2.8.1 Infix to Postfix conversion

Converting from Infix Notation to Postfix Notation by Hand

To convert an infix expression to postfix, you simply place each operator in the infix expression immediately to the right of its respective right parenthesis. Then you rewrite the expression in the new order, and what you get is the same expression in prefix notation.

The first thing you need to do is fully parenthesize the expression.

Example: $(3 + 6) * (2 - 4) + 7$

after parenthesizing becomes $(((3 + 6) * (2 - 4)) + 7)$.

Now, move each of the operators immediately to the right of their respective right parentheses.

$$(((3 + 6) * (2 - 4)) + 7)$$

becomes 3 6 + 2 4 - * 7 +

Converting from Infix Notation to Postfix Notation by using Stack

To convert infix expression to postfix expression, use the **Stack** data structure. Scan the infix expression from left to right. Whenever we get an operand, add it to the postfix expression and if we get an operator or parenthesis add it to the stack by maintaining their precedence.

Algorithm : InfixToPostfix

Input :   Q is an arithmetic expression in infix notation.
Output :   P is an arithmetic expression in postfix notation.
Data structure : Array representation of stack with Top as pointer. **X** represents any operator

```
Step 1: PUSH left parenthesis "("  into stack and
            add right parenthesis ")" at the end of Q.

Step 2: Scan the expression Q from Left to Right and
        repeat the step 3 to 6 for each element of Q till stack empty.

Step 3: If an operand occurs add it to P.

Step 4: If a Left parenthesis occurs then PUSH  it to stack

Step 5: If an operator X occurs then

            A: Repeatedly POP the stack and add to P, each operator
               which has same or higher precedence than X
            B: Add X to stack

Step 6: If a Right parenthesis occurs then

            A: Repeatedly POP from stack and add to P each operator
               until a left parenthesis occurs.
            B: Remove the left parenthesis
Step 7: Exit
```

Example: Q = A + (B * C - (D / E ^F) * G) * H

Add right parenthesis at the end of the expression
$$Q = A + (B * C - (D / E \; \hat{} \, F) * G) * H)$$

Symbol Scanned	Stack	p
	(	
A	(	A
+	(+	A
(	(+ (	A
B	(+ (	AB
*	(+ (*	AB
C	(+ (*	ABC
-	(+ (-	ABC*
(	(+ (- (	ABC*
D	(+ (- (	ABC*D
/	(+ (- (/	ABC*D
E	(+ (- (/	ABC*DE
^	(+ (- (/ ^	ABC*DE
F	(+ (- (/ ^	ABC*DEF
)	(+ (-	ABC*DEF ^ /
*	(+ (- *	ABC*DEF ^ /
G	(+ (- *	ABC*DEF ^ /G
)	(+	ABC*DEF ^ /G * -
*	(+ *	ABC*DEF ^ /G * -
H	(+ *	ABC*DEF ^ /G * - H
)		ABC*DEF ^ /G * - H * +

The postfix expression is ABC*DEF ^/G * - H * +

2.8.2   Postfix Expression Evaluation

Algorithm : Postfix Expression Evaluation
Input :   P is an arithmetic expression in Postfix notation.
Output :   Value is the expression evaluated.
Data structure : Array representation of stack with Top as pointer. **X** represents any operator

```
Step 1: Add ")" at the end of P
Step 2: Scan P from left to right and repeat the steps 3 and 4
Step 3: If an operand occurs, PUSH it to stack.
Step 4: If an operator X occurs, then
           (i): Remove the top elements of the stack.
                   Where A is the top element and
                     B is the next top element
         (ii): Evaluate B X A
         (iii): Push the result of step (ii) back to stack
Step 5: Set the value equals to TOP element of the stack.
```

Example : Evaluate the expression $5 * (6 + 2) - 12 / 4$
Add ") " at the end of P
$$P = 5 \ 6 \ 2 + * \ 12 \ 4 \ / -)$$

Scanned Symbol	Stack
5	5
6	5, 6
2	5, 6, 2
+	5, 8
*	40
12	40, 12
4	40, 12, 4
/	40, 3
-	37

The Value after evaluation is 37, which is on Top of Stack.

2.9 Searching Algorithms

1. Linear search:
     Small and unsorted arrays

2. Binary search:
     Large arrays and sorted arrays

2.9.1 Linear Search

It means looking at each element of the array, in turn, until you find the target
value.
Algorithm

```
1. Start
2. Read the ITEM to be searched
3. Set flag=0
4. Repeat for i=0 to N-1
5.          if  A[i]= =ITEM
6.                  print "ITEM found"
7.                  flag=1
8. If flag= =0
9.          print "ITEM not found"
```

- In the best case, the target value is the first element of the array. So, the
  search takes a constant amount of time. Computer scientists denote this
  $O(1)$ In real life, we don't care about the best case, because it so rarely
  actually happens.

- In the worst case, the target value is in the last element of the array. So,
  the search takes an amount of time proportional to the length of the array.
  Computer scientists denote this $O(n)$

- In the average case, the target value is somewhere in the array. So, on
  average, the target value will be in the middle of the array. So the search
  takes an amount of time proportional to half the length of the array $n/2$ also
  proportional to the length of the array – $O(n)$ again

2.9.2 Binary Search

The initial search region is the whole array. Compare ITEM with data value in
the middle of the search region. If target is found, stop else check if ITEM is less
than the middle data value, the new search region is the lower half of the data. If
ITEM is greater than the middle data value, the new search region is the higher
half of the data. And the process continues either till ITEM found or till the array
is exhausted.

Algorithm

Let A be a sorted array with N elements

```
1. Start
2. Read the ITEM to be searched
3. Set beg=0, end=n-1
4. Repeat steps 5 to 10 while(beg<=end )
5.        mid=(beg+end)/2
6.   if (A[mid] = = ITEM) , goto 11
7.       if ITEM< A[mid] then
8.               set end=mid-1
9.          else
10.                  beg=mid+1
11.  If A[mid]=ITEM then
12.               print "item found"
13. Else print "element not found"
```

Time Complexity of Binary Search Algorithm

- **Best case Time Complexity** of Binary Search Algorithm is when the element is at the middle index of the array. It takes only one comparison to find the target element. So the best case complexity is $O(1)$..

- **Average Case Time Complexity** of Binary Search Algorithm: $O(\log N)$

Consider an array Arr[] of length N and element X to be found. There can be two cases:

Case1: Element is present in the array

Case2: Element is not present in the array

There are N Case1 and 1 Case2. So total number of cases = N+1. Now notice the following:

An element at index $N/2$ can be found in 1 comparison Elements at index $N/4$ and $3N/4$ can be found in 2 comparisons. Elements at indices $N/8$, $3N/8$, $5N/8$ and $7N/8$ can be found in 3 comparisons and so on.

Based on this we can conclude that elements that require:

1 comparison = 1

2 comparisons = 2

3 comparisons = 4

x comparisons = 2^{x-1}

where x belongs to the range $[1, \log N]$ because maximum comparisons = maximum time N can be halved = maximum comparisons to reach 1st element = $\log N$.

So, total comparisons
= 1*(elements requiring 1 comparisons) + 2*(elements requiring 2 comparisons) + . . . + logN*(elements requiring logN comparisons)   = 1*1 + 2*2 + 3*4 + . . . + logN * (2logN-1)   = 2logN * (logN − 1) + 1   = N * (logN − 1) + 1

Total number of cases = N+1.

Therefore, the average complexity =
(N*(logN − 1) + 1)/N+1 = N*logN / (N+1) + 1/(N+1).
Here the dominant term is N*logN/(N+1) which is approximately logN. So the average case complexity is O(logN).

- **Worst Case Time Complexity** of Binary Search Algorithm: O(log N)
  The worst case will be when the element is present in the first position. As seen in the average case, the comparison required to reach the first element is logN. So, the time complexity for the worst case is O(logN).

Module 3

3.1   Linked List

A linked list is an ordered collection of finite, homogeneous data elements called nodes where the linear order is maintained by means of links or pointers. A linked list is a dynamic data structure where the amount of memory required can be varied during its use.

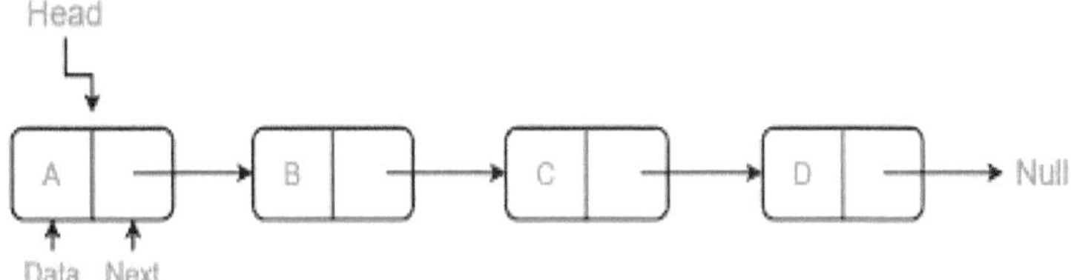

Figure 3.1: Linked List

Advantages of Linked List

- Dynamic Data structure: The size of memory can be allocated or de-allocated at run time based on the operation insertion or deletion.

- Ease of Insertion/Deletion: The insertion and deletion of elements are simpler than arrays since no elements need to be shifted after insertion and deletion, Just the address needed to be updated.

- Efficient Memory Utilization: As we know Linked List is a dynamic data structure the size increases or decreases as per the requirement so this avoids the wastage of memory.

3.1.1 Self-Referential Structures

A structure can have members which point to a structure variable of the same type. These types of structures are called self-referential structures and are widely used in dynamic data structures like trees, linked list, etc. The following is a definition of a self-referential structure.

```
struct node
{
int data;
struct node *next;
};
```
   Here, next is a pointer to a struct node variable.

In the linked list, the adjacency between the elements is maintained by means of links or pointers. A link or pointer actually is the address (memory location) of the subsequent element. An element in a linked list is a specially termed node, which can be viewed as shown in the figure.
A node consists of two fields: DATA (to store the actual information) and NEXT (to point to the next node)

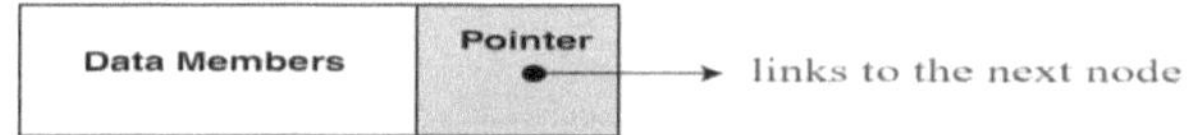

Figure 3.2: Structure of a Node

A linked list is called "linked" because each node in the series has a pointer that points to the next node in the list.

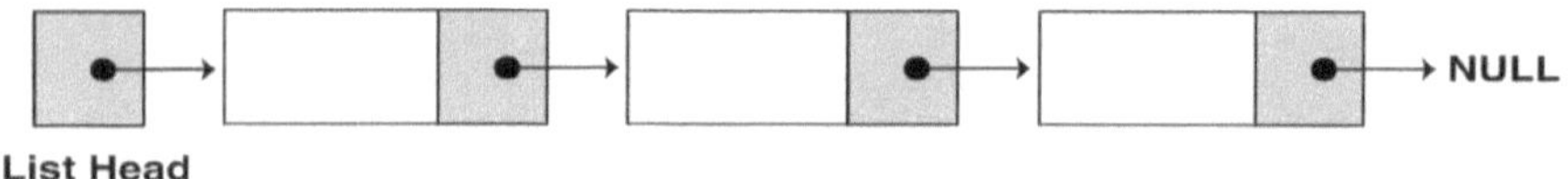

Figure 3.3: Structure of a Linked List

Head: pointer to the first node.
The Next field of the Last node points to **NULL**.

Depending on the requirements, the pointers are maintained and accordingly the Linked list can be classified int three major groups.

1. Single linked list.

2. Double linked list.

3. Circular linked list.

3.1.2   Dynamic Memory allocation

Dynamic memory allocation is also known as Runtime memory allocation because
the memory is allocated during runtime or program execution. The allocation and
release of the memory space can be done using the library functions of stdlib.h
header file. These functions allocate memory from a memory area called heap and
deallocate this memory whenever not required so that it can be used for some
other purpose.

Properties of Dynamic Memory allocation

- Memory is allocated at runtime.

- Memory can be allocated and released at any time.

- Heap memory is used here.

- Dynamic memory allocation is slow.

- It is more efficient as compared to Static memory allocation

- The allocation process is simple is complicated.

- Memory can be resized dynamically or reused.

The library functions of the stdlib.h header file in C programming Language,
which helps to allocate memory dynamically are.

* malloc()
* calloc()
* realloc()
* free()

1. malloc()
   This function is used to allocate the single block of requested memory. On
   Success, the malloc() function returns a pointer to the first byte of the allocated memory. The malloc() function gives a NULL output when the
   memory is not enough.

   Syntax: ptr=(data _type *)malloc(specified _size)

   Here in the above syntax, ptr is a pointer of type data_type, and specified_size
   is the size in bytes required to allocate. The cast (data_type *) typecast the
   pointer returned by the malloc() function.

   Example

   ptr = (int*)malloc(100);
   In the above example, the statement allocates 100 bytes of memory space,
   and the pointer variable ptr stores the address of the first byte in the memory.

2. calloc()

The calloc() function is used to allocate the memory as a number of elements of a given size. The calloc() function is similar to malloc() function. The only difference is that it takes two argument values. The first argument specifies the number of data items for which space is required, and the second argument specifies the size of each data item.

Syntax: ptr=(data _type *)calloc(n, specified_size)

Here in the above syntax, ptr is a pointer of type data_type, n is the number of data items, and specified_size is the size in bytes required to allocate. The cast (data_type *) typecast the pointer returned by the malloc() function.

Example

ptr = (int*)calloc(4, sizeof (int));
In the above example, the statement allocates four blocks of memory, each block contains 4 bytes, and the starting address is stored in the pointer variable ptr.

3. realloc()

The realloc() function is used to increase the memory allocated by malloc() or calloc() function. This function alters the size of the memory block without losing the old data. The realloc() function takes two argument values. The first argument is a pointer variable to the block of memory that was previously allocated by calloc() or malloc(), and the second argument is the new size for that memory block.

Syntax: realloc(pointer_variable, n);

Here in the above syntax, pointer_variable is a pointer to the block of memory that was previously allocated by malloc() or calloc() function, and n is the new size for that memory block.

Example

int *ptr;
ptr = (int*)malloc(100);
ptr = (int*)realloc(ptr, 400);
Here in the above example, we increased memory size from 100 bytes to 400 bytes.

4. free()

When memory is allocated dynamically by the malloc() and calloc() function, it should always be released when it is no longer required. Otherwise, it will consume memory until the program exit. The free() function is used to release this allocated memory space.

Syntax: free(pointer_variable);

Here the memory block pointed by the pointer 'pointer_variable' would be released back to the system.

3.1.3   Singly Linked List

In any single linked list, every "Node" contains two fields, data and link. The data field is used to store actual value of that node and Next field is used to store the address of the next node in the sequence. Each node contains only one link which points to the subsequent node in the list. The header node points to the 1st node in the list The Next field of the last node contain NULL value. Here one can move from left to right only. So, it is also called one-way list. Traversing a singly linked list is done in a forward direction.

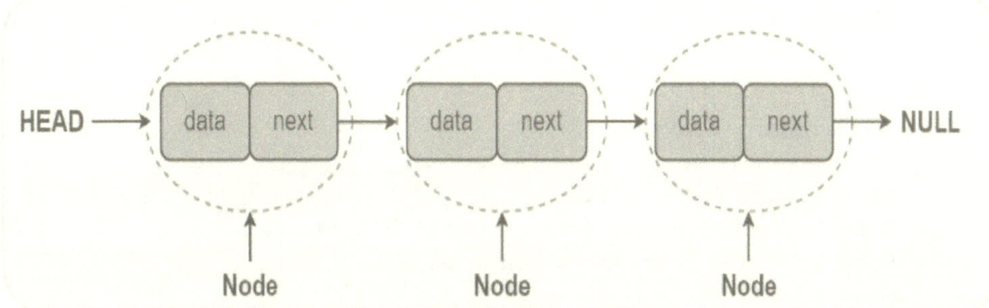

Figure 3.4: Single Linked List

Dynamic Representation of Linked List

The efficient way of representing a linked list is using the free pool of storage which has

- memory bank : Collection of free memory spaces

- memory manager: a program

Whenever a node is required, the request is placed to the memory manager. It will search the memory bank for the block. If found, it will be granted.

Garbage collector: Another program that returns the unused node to the memory bank.

Disadvantages of Linked Lists

- Random Access: Unlike arrays, linked lists do not allow direct access to elements by index. Traversal is required to reach a specific node.

- Extra Memory: Linked lists require additional memory for storing the pointers, compared to arrays.

3.1.4   Operations on a Single Linked List

* Traversing the list

* Inserting a node into the list

* Deleting a node from the list

* Merging the list with another to make a larger list

1. Traversing a Linked List

Traversing is the most common operation that is performed in almost every scenario of singly linked list. Traversing means visiting each node of the list once in order to perform some operation on that.

Algorithm : Traverse

```
Step 1: SET PTR = START
Step 2: Repeat Steps 3 and 4 while PTR != NULL
Step 3: Apply Process to PTR-> DATA
Step 4: SET PTR = PTR-> NEXT
          [END OF LOOP]
Step 5: RETURN
```

Some uses of Traversing is to display the contents of the linked list, count the number of nodes and also search for a key in a Linked List.

Algorithm : Search for a key

```
Step 1: SET PTR = START
Step 2: SET FLAG=0
Step 3: Repeat Step 4 while PTR != NULL
Step 4: IF KEY = PTR -> DATA
              SET FLAG = 1
              Go To Step 5
          ELSE
              SET PTR = PTR->NEXT
          [END OF IF]
        [END OF LOOP]
Step 5: RETURN FLAG
```

Algorithm : Count nodes

```
Step 1: SET COUNT= 0
Step 2: SET PTR = START
```

```
Step 3: Repeat Steps 4 and 5 while PTR != NULL
Step 4: SET COUNT = COUNT + 1
Step 5: SET PTR = PTR-> NEXT
           [END OF LOOP]
Step 6: Write COUNT
Step 7: RETURN
```

2. Inserting a node into the list

- The new node is inserted at the beginning.

- The new node is inserted at the end.

- The new node is inserted after a given node.

- The new node is inserted at a position

Case 1: Insert at beginning
To insert a node at the front of a Linked List:

Make the Next field of new node of point to first node.
Remove the head from the original first node of Linked List.
Make the Head of the Linked List to point to new node.

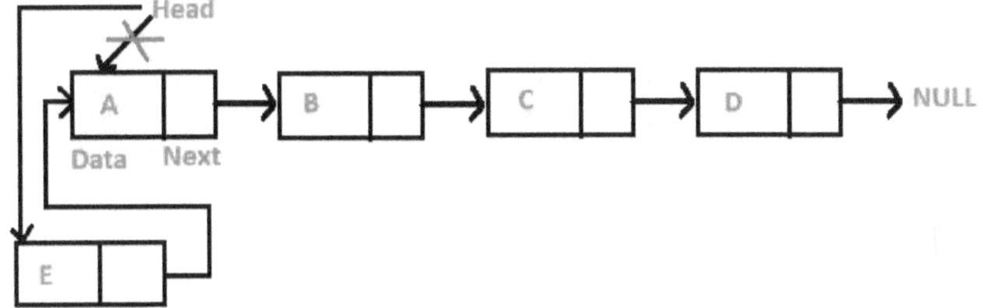

Figure 3.5: Insert Node at beginning

Algorithm: Insert at beg

```
Step 1: NEW = getNode (AVAIL)
Step 2: IF NEW = NULL
           Write UNDERFLOW
Step 3: ELSE
Step 4:         NEW-> DATA = ITEM
Step 5:         NEW-> NEXT= NULL
Step 6:         IF START==NULL
Step 7:            START = NEW
```

```
Step 8:          ELSE
Step 9:             NEW->NEXT=START
Step 10:            START = NEW
              [End if]
        [End if]
Step 11: RETURN
```

Case 2: Insert at end

To insert a node at the end of a Linked List:

> Go to the last node of the Linked List by traversing.
> Change the next field of last node from NULL to the new node.
> Make the ptr of new node as NULL to show the end of Linked List.

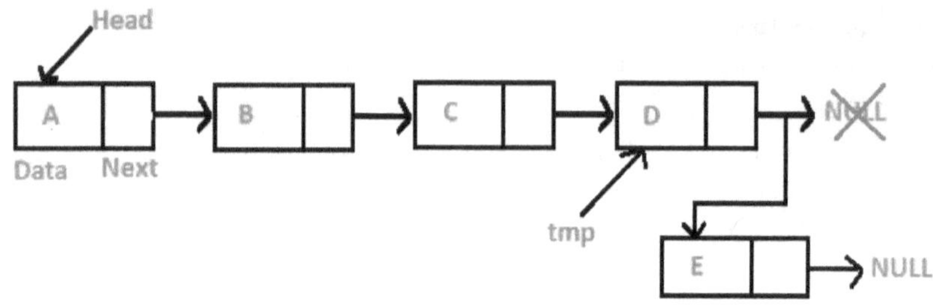

Figure 3.6: Insert Node at end

Algorithm: Insert at end

```
Step 1: NEW = getNode (AVAIL)
Step 2: IF NEW = NULL
           Write UNDERFLOW
Step 3: ELSE
Step 4:          NEW-> DATA = ITEM
Step 5:          NEW-> NEXT= NULL
Step 6:          IF START==NULL
Step 7:             START = NEW
Step 8:          ELSE
Step 9:              Set PTR=START
Step 10:  Repeat step 11 While PTR->NEXT !=NULL
Step 11:        PTR=PTR->NEXT
                [END OF LOOP]
Step 12:  PTR->NEXT=NEW
              [End if]
          [End if]
Step 13: RETURN
```

Case 3: Insert after a node
To insert a node after a given node in a Linked List:

Check if the given node exists or not. If it does not exists, terminate the process.
If the given node exists,
    Make the element to be inserted as a new node.
    Copy the next field of given node to the new node.   Now change the next field of tmp to point to the new node.

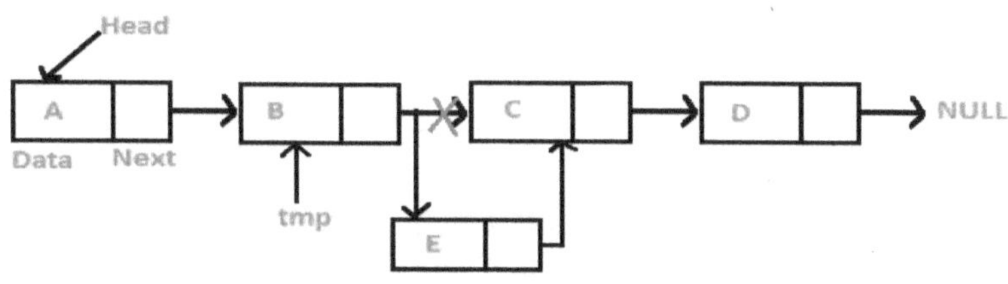

Figure 3.7: Insert Node after a given node

Algorithm: Insert after a node

```
Step 1: NEW = getNode (AVAIL)
Step 2: IF NEW= NULL
Step 3:         Write UNDERFLOW
Step 4: ELSE
Step 5:            NEW-> DATA = ITEM
Step 6:            NEW-> NEXT = NULL
Step 7:         SET PTR = START
Step 8:         Repeat Steps 9
                    while PTR -> DATA != KEY and  PTR !=NULL
Step 9:             SET PTR = PTR -> NEXT
            [END OF LOOP]
Step 10: IF PTR->DATA!= KEY
Step 11:           WRITE KEY NOT AVAILABLE, GOTO  14
Step 12: SET NEW-> NEXT = PTR->NEXT
Step 13: PTR->NEXT = NEW
Step 14: Return
```

Case 4: Insert at a position

To insert a node after a given node in a Linked List, we traverse till node at
$pos - 1$, pos is the location to insert the new node.
Refer to figure 3.7, pos stops at position of tmp in figure Check if the given
position exceeds the length or not. If so, terminate the process.
If the given position< length then,

Make the element to be inserted as a new node.

Copy the next field of temp node at $pos - 1$ to the new node.

Now change the next pointer of tmp node to point to new node.

Algorithm: Insert at a pos

```
Step 1: NEW = getNode (AVAIL)
Step 2: IF NEW= NULL
                Write UNDERFLOW
                Go to Step 10
          [END OF IF]
Step 3: NEW-> DATA = ITEM
Step 4: NEW-> NEXT = NULL
Step 4: SET PTR = START AND  i=1
Step 5: Repeat Steps 6 while
                i<POS-1 and  PTR !=NULL
Step 6:   SET PTR = PTR -> LINK
Step 7:     i=i+1
          [END OF LOOP]
Step 8: IF PTR== NULL
          WRITE "Position exceeds list",GOTO  11
Step 9: SET NEW-> LINK = PTR->LINK
Step 10: PTR->LINK = NEW
Step 11: Return
```

3. Deleting a node from the list

- Delete node at the beginning.

- Delete node at the end.

- Delete given node

Case 1: Delete node at the beginning

To delete a node from the front of a Linked List:

Set ptr point to first node.
Change Head point to second node of Linked List.

Free memory for the node to be deleted.

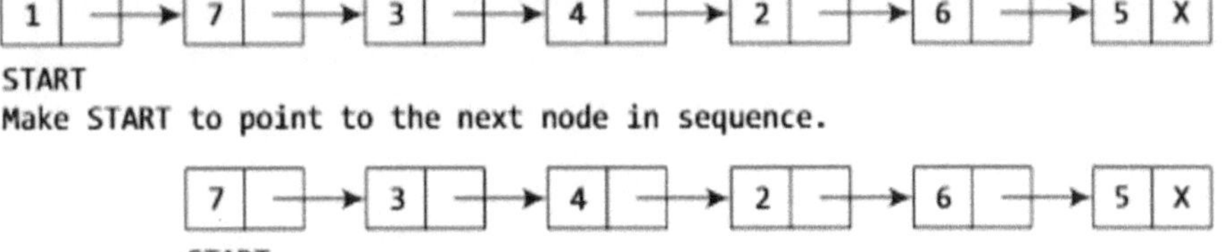

Figure 3.8: Delete Node at beginning

Algorithm: Delete at beg

```
Step 1: IF START = NULL
                Write UNDERFLOW
                Go to Step 5
          [END OF IF]
Step 2: SET PTR = START
Step 3: SET START = PTR-> NEXT
Step 4: FREE PTR
Step 5: Return
```

Case 2: Delete node at the end

To delete a node from the end of a Linked List. we use two pointers, ptr is a pointer that points to current node and preptr points to node before ptr.

Take pointer variables PTR and PREPTR which initially point to START.

Move PTR and PREPTR such that NEXT part of PTR = NULL. PREPTR always points to the node just before the node pointed by PTR.

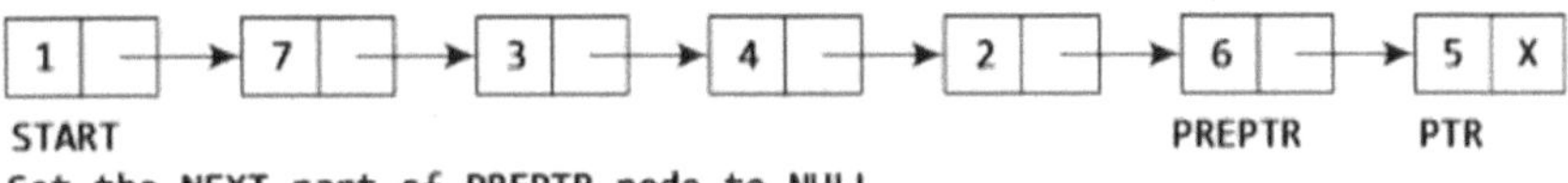

Set the NEXT part of PREPTR node to NULL.

Figure 3.9: Delete Node at the End

Set ptr and preptr point to first node.
Traverse to second last element.
Change its next pointer to null.
Free memory for the node to be deleted.

Algorithm: Delete at end

```
Step 1: IF START = NULL
               Write UNDERFLOW
                Go to Step 8
          [END IF]
Step 2: SET PTR = START
Step 3: Repeat Steps 4 and 5 while PTR -> NEXT != NULL
Step 4: SET PREPTR = PTR
Step 5: SET PTR = PTR ->NEXT
        [END OF LOOP]
Step 6: SET PREPTR ->NEXT = NULL
Step 7: FREE PTR
Step 8: Return
```

Case 3: Delete a given node

Set ptr point to first node.
Traverse the linked list from the head node until the node to be deleted is found.
If the node to be deleted is not found, return NULL.
Otherwise, set the previous node's next pointer to the node after the node to be deleted. Free memory for the node to be deleted.

Take pointer variables PTR and PREPTR which initially point to START.

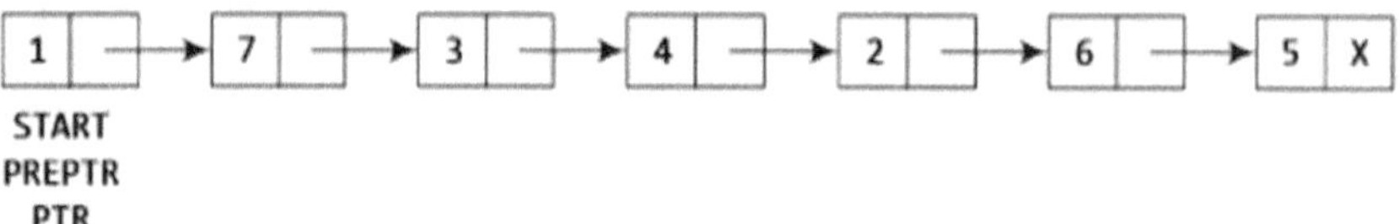

Set the NEXT part of PREPTR to the NEXT part of PTR.

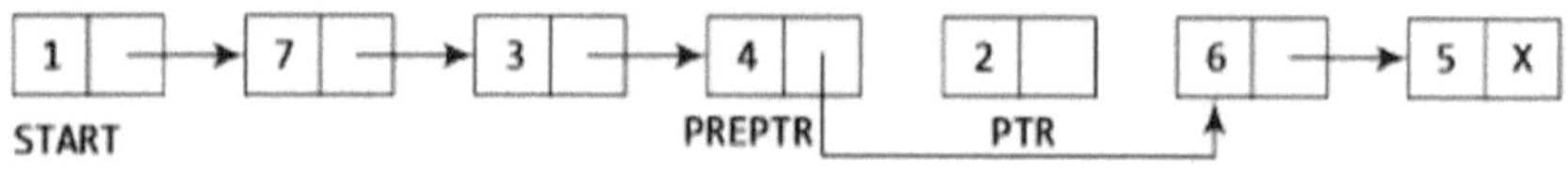

Figure 3.10: Delete Given Node

Algorithm: Delete given node

```
Step 1: IF START = NULL
Step 2:        Write UNDERFLOW, Goto 11
        [END IF]
Step 3: SET PTR = START
Step 4: Repeat 5,6 while PTR->DATA != KEY and PTR!=NULL
Step 5: SET PREPTR = PTR
Step 6: SET PTR = PTR->LINK
        [END OF LOOP]
Step 7: if (PTR->DATA==KEY)
Step 7: SET PREPTR->LINK = PTR->LINK
Step 8: FREE PTR
Step 9: else
Step 10:print "KEY NOT FOUND"
   [END OF IF]
   [END OF IF]
Step 11: RETURN
```

4. Merging two Linked list

Given two linked lists consisting of N and M nodes respectively. The task is to merge both of the lists (in place) and return the head of the merged list. Let H1 and H2 be the Head pointers such that one will point to list1 and another will point to list2 respectively.

Now traverse the lists till one of them reaches the end.

Then make the Next field of the last node point to the first node of the list2. return the head node of list 2 as it is not required.

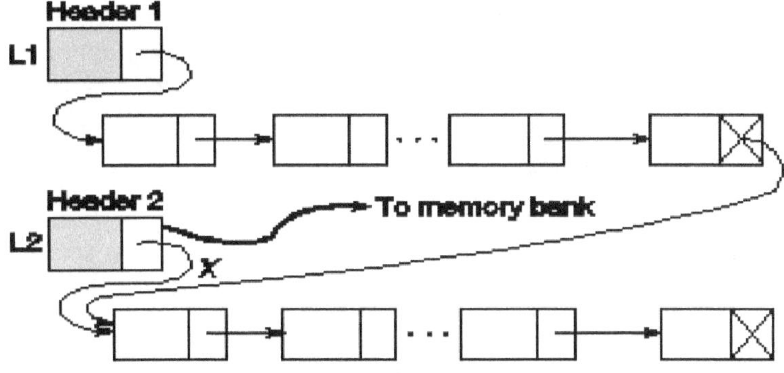

Figure 3.11: Merge two Lists

Algorithm: Merge two Lists

```
Step 1: Set PTR=H1
Step 2: Repeat step 3 While PTR->NEXT !=NULL
Step 3:         PTR=PTR->NEXT
        [End Loop]
Step 4: PTR-> NEXT= H2
Step 5: RETURN H2
```

Merging two sorted List Given two sorted linked lists ,merge both of the lists (in place) and return the head of the merged list. First, make a H3 node for the new merged linked list.Now make two pointers ptr1 and pt2, one will point to list1 and another will point to list2. Now traverse the lists till one of them gets exhausted. If the value of the node pointing to either list is smaller than another, add that smaller node to the merged list and increment that pointer of the list. If one list is exhausted, copy the remaining elements of the other list.

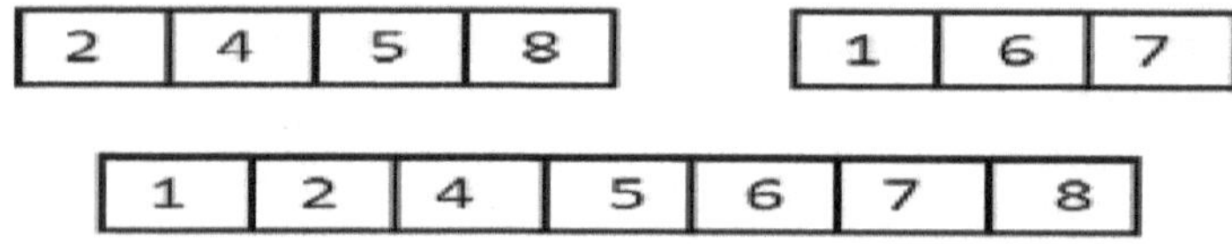

Figure 3.12: Merge two sorted Lists

Comparison of Array and LinkedList

ARRAY	LINKED LIST
Size of an array is fixed	Size of a list is not fixed
Memory is allocated from stack	Memory is allocated from heap
It is necessary to specify the number of elements during declaration (i.e., during compile time).	It is not necessary to specify the number of elements during declaration (i.e., memory is allocated during run time).
It occupies less memory than a linked list for the same number of elements.	It occupies more memory.
Inserting new elements at the front is potentially expensive because existing elements need to be shifted over to make room.	Inserting a new element at any position can be carried out easily.

3.1.5   Doubly Linked List

A doubly linked list is a two- way list with a linear collection of data elements
called nodes. Each node contains references to both the next and previous nodes.
This allows for traversal in both forward and backward directions, but it requires
additional memory for the backward reference.
Each node N is divided in to three parts

- Data field contains the data of N.

- LLINK field contains the pointer to the preceding Node in the list.

- RLINK field contains the pointer to the next node in the list.

The data field is used to store actual value of that node and LLINK field is
used to store the address of the previous node in the sequence. RLINK field is
used to store the address of the next node in the sequence.
The Head points to the 1st node in the list and the Tail points to the last node
in the list. The LLINK field of the first node contain NULL value. The RLINK
field of the last node contain NULL value. Here one can move from left to right
only from front using head node, and also from right to left from the last node.
So, it is also called two-way list. Traversing a doubly linked list can be done in
both directions, forward direction and backward direction.

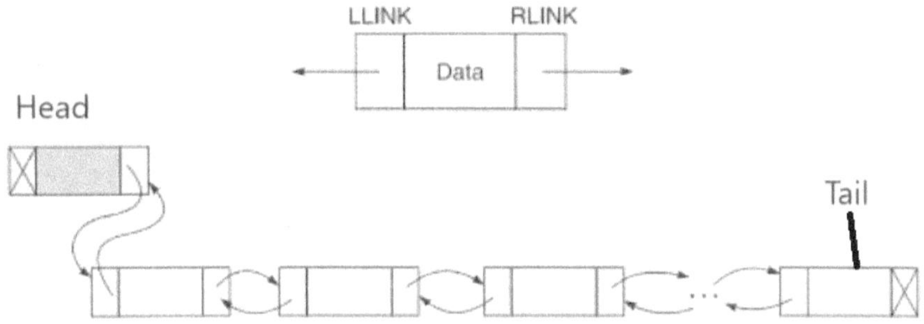

Figure 3.13: Doubly Linked List

```
struct node
{
int DATA;
struct node *LLINK;
struct node *RLINK;
};
```

```
LLINK and RLINK are pointers, that point to another node.
```

3.1.6   Operations on a Doubly Linked List

* Traversing the list

* Inserting a node into the list

* Deleting a node from the list

* Merging the list with another to make a larger list

1. Traversing a Linked List

Traversing is the most common operation that is performed in almost every scenario of a linked list. Traversing means visiting each node of the list once in order to perform some operation on that. Here we can traverse in both directions.

Algorithm : TraverseForward

```
Step 1: SET PTR = HEAD
Step 2: Repeat Steps 3 and 4 while PTR != NULL
Step 3: Apply Process to PTR-> DATA
Step 4: SET PTR = PTR-> RLINK
          [END OF LOOP]
Step 5: RETURN
```

We can also traverse in the reverse direction, starting with the tail.

Algorithm : TraverseBackward

```
Step 1: SET PTR = TAIL
Step 2: Repeat Steps 3 and 4 while PTR != NULL
Step 3: Apply Process to PTR-> DATA
Step 4: SET PTR = PTR-> LLINK
          [END OF LOOP]
Step 5: RETURN
```

2. Inserting a node into the list

   - The new node is inserted at the beginning.

   - The new node is inserted at the end.

   - The new node is inserted after a given node.

   - The new node is inserted at a position

Case 1: Insert at beginning

To insert a node at the front of a doubly Linked List:

Make the Next field of new node of point to first node.
Remove the head from the original first node of Linked List.
Make the Head of the Linked List to point to new node.

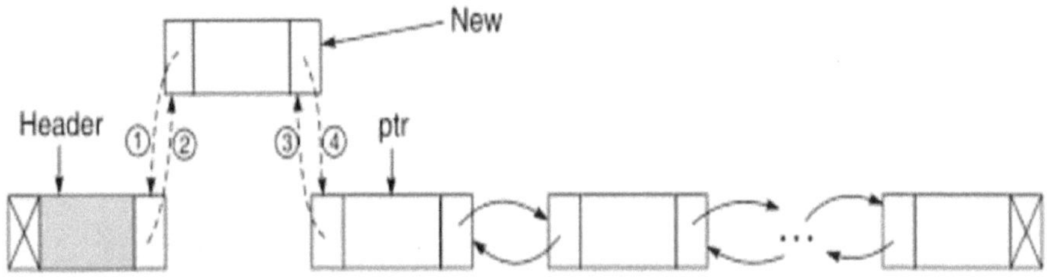

Figure 3.14: Insert Node at beginning

1. ptr = HEADER→RLINK   // Points to the first node
2. new = **GetNode**(NODE)   // Avail a new node from the memory bank
3. **If** (new ≠ NULL) then   // If new node is available
4.   new→LLINK = HEADER   // Newly inserted node points the header as 1 in Figure
5.   HEADER→RLINK = new   // Header now points to then new node as 2 in Figure
6.   new→RLINK = ptr   // See the change in pointer shown as 3 in Figure
7.   ptr→LLINK = new   // See the change in pointer shown as 4 in Figure
8.   new→DATA = X   // Copy the data into the newly inserted node
9. **Else**
10.   **Print** "Unable to allocate memory: Insertion is not possible"
11. **EndIf**

Case 2: Insert at end

To insert a node at the end of a Linked List:

Go to the last node of the Linked List by traversing.
Change the next field of last node from NULL to the new node.
Make the ptr of new node as NULL to show the end of Linked List.

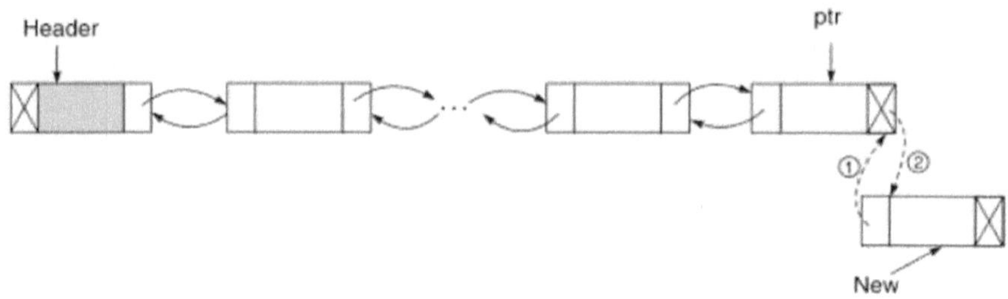

Figure 3.15: Insert Node at end

1. ptr = HEADER
2. **While** (ptr→RLINK ≠ NULL) **do**   // Move to the last node
3.   ptr = ptr→RLINK
4. **EndWhile**
5. new = **GetNode**(NODE)   // Avail a new node
6. **If** (new ≠ NULL) **then**   // If the node is available
7.   new→LLINK = ptr   // Change the pointer shown as 1 in Figure
8.   ptr→RLINK = new   // Change the pointer shown as 2 in Figure
9.   new→RLINK = NULL   // Make the new node as the last node
10.   new→.DATA = X   // Copy the data into the new node
11. **Else**
12.   **Print** "Unable to allocate memory: Insertion is not possible"
13. **EndIf**

Case 3: Insert after a node

To insert a node after a given node in a Linked List:

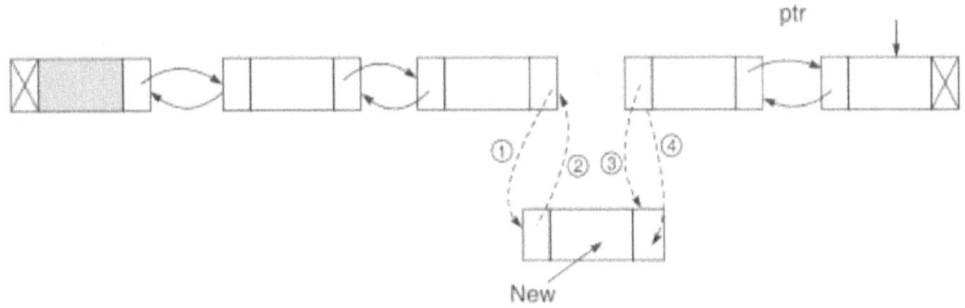

Figure 3.16: Insert Node after a given node

1. ptr = HEADER
2. **While** (ptr→DATA ≠ KEY) and (ptr→RLINK ≠ NULL)   // Move to the key node if the
                                // current node is not the KEY node or if the list reaches the end
3.   ptr = ptr→RLINK
4. **EndWhile**
5. new = GetNode(NODE)   // Get a new node from the pool of free storage
6. **If** (new = NULL) **then**   // When the memory is not available
7.   **Print** (Memory is not available)
8.   **Exit**   // Quit the program
9. **EndIf**
10. **If** (ptr→RLINK = NULL) **then**   // If the KEY is not found in the list
11.   new→LLINK = ptr
12.   ptr→RLINK = new   // Insert at the end
13.   new→RLINK = NULL
14.   new→DATA = X // Copy the information to the newly inserted node
15. **Else**   // The KEY is available
16.   ptr1 = ptr→RLINK   // Next node after the key node
17.   new→LLINK = ptr   // Change the pointer shown as 2 in Figure
18.   new→RLINK = ptr1   // Change the pointer shown as 4 in Figure
19.   ptr→RLINK = new   // Change the pointer shown as 1 in Figure
20.   ptr1→LLINK = new   // Change the pointer shown as 3 in Figure
21.   ptr = new   // This becomes the current node
22.   new→DATA = X // Copy the content to the newly inserted node
23. **EndIf**

3. Deleting a node from the list

- - Delete node at the beginning.

- - Delete node at the end.

- - Delete given node

Case 1: Delete node at the beginning

To delete a node from the front of a Linked List:

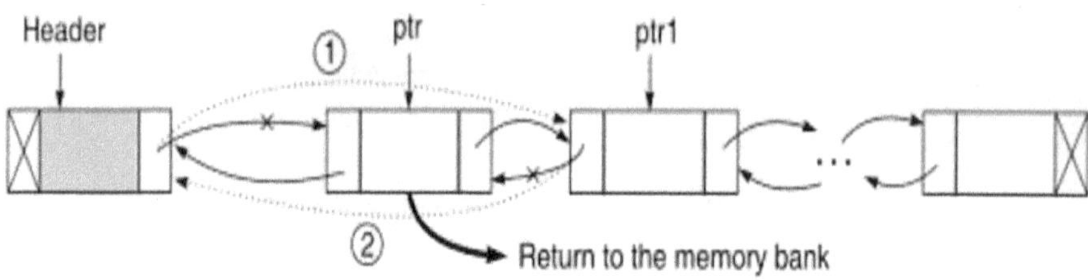

Figure 3.17: Delete Node at beginning

1. ptr = HEADER→RLINK   // Pointer to the first node
2. **If** (ptr = NULL) **then**   // If the list is empty
3.   **Print** "List is empty: No deletion is made"
4.   **Exit**
5. **Else**
6.   ptr1 = ptr→RLINK   // Pointer to the second node
7.   HEADER→RLINK = ptr1   // Change the pointer shown as 1 in Figure
8.   **If** (ptr1 ≠ NULL)   // If the list contains a node after the first node of deletion
9.   ptr1→LLINK = HEADER   // Change the pointer shown as 2 in Figure
10.   **EndIf**
11.   **ReturnNode** (ptr)   // Return the deleted node to the memory bank
12. **EndIf**

Case 2: Delete node at the end

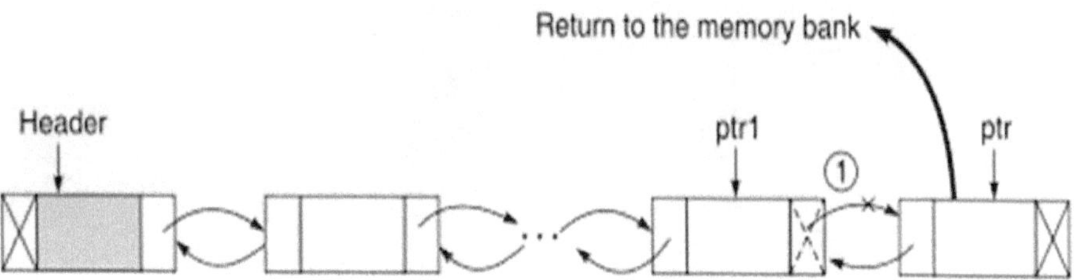

Figure 3.18: Delete Node at end

1. ptr = HEADER
2. **While** (ptr→RLINK ≠ NULL) **do**   // Move to the last node
3.   ptr = ptr→RLINK
4. **EndWhile**
5. **If** (ptr = HEADER) **then**   // If the list is empty
6.   **Print** "List is empty: No deletion is made"
7.   **Exit**   // Quit the program
8. **Else**
9.   ptr1 = ptr→LLINK   // Pointer to the last but one node
10.   ptr1→RLINK = NULL   // Change the pointer shown as 1 in Figure
11.   **ReturnNode** (ptr)   // Return the deleted node to the memory bank
12. **EndIf**

Case 3: Delete a given node

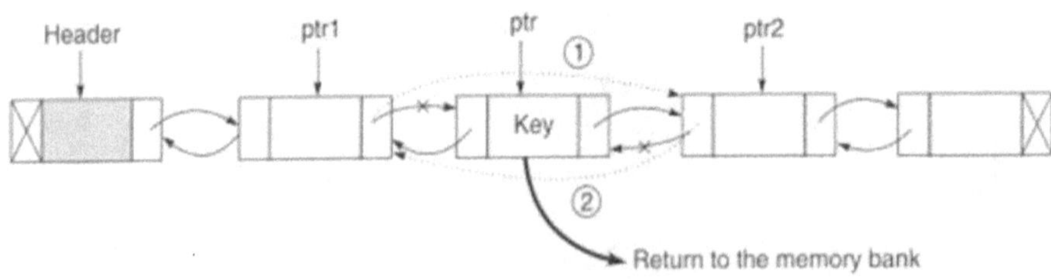

Figure 3.19: Delete Given Node

1. ptr = HEADER→RLINK   // Move to the first node
2. **If** (ptr = NULL) **then**
3.   Print "List is empty: No deletion is made"
4.   Exit
5. **EndIf**   // Quit the program
6. **While** (ptr→DATA ≠ KEY) and (ptr→RLINK ≠ NULL) **do** // Move to the desired node
7.   ptr = ptr→RLINK
8. **EndWhile**
9. **If** (ptr→DATA = KEY) **then**   // If the node is found
10.   ptr1 = ptr→LLINK   // Track the predecessor node
11.   ptr2 = ptr→RLINK   // Track the successor node
12.   ptr1→RLINK = ptr2   // Change the pointer shown as 1 in Figure
13.   **If** (ptr2 ≠ NULL) **then**   // If the deleted node is the last node
14.   ptr2→LLINK = ptr1   // Change the pointer shown as 2 in Figure
15.   **EndIf**
16.   **ReturnNode**(ptr)   // Return the free node to the memory bank
17. **Else**
18.   **Print** "The node does not exist in the given list"
19. **EndIf**

3.1.7 Circular Linked List

In a single linked list, the link field of the last node is null. If we utilize this link field to store the pointer of the header node, a number of advantages can be gained. A linked list, whose last node points back to the header node, instead of containing the null pointer is called a circular list.

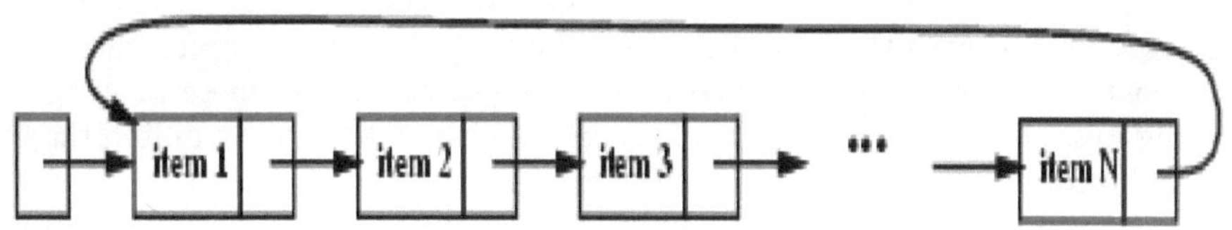

Figure 3.20: Circular Linked List

Algorithm : Search for a key

```
Step 1: SET PTR = HEAD
Step 2: SET FLAG = 0
Step 3: IF KEY = PTR->DATA
                SET FLAG = 1
                Go To Step 5
          ELSE
                SET PTR = PTR->NEXT
          [END OF IF]
Step 4: Repeat Step 3 while PTR != HEAD

          [END OF DO WHILE LOOP]
Step 5: RETURN FLAG
```

Advantages:

- Accessibility of a member node – here every member node is accessible from any node by merely chaining through the list eg: Finding of earlier occurrence or post occurrence of a data will be easy

- Null link problem- Null value in next field may create problem during the execution of the program if proper care is not taken

- Some easy-to-implement operations - Operations like merging, splitting, deletion, dispose of an entire list etc. can be done easily with circular list

Disadvantages:

- If not cared system may get trap into in infinite loop.

- It occurs when we are unable to detect the end of the list while moving from one node to the next

- Solution: Special node can be maintained with data part as NULL and this node does not contain any valid information. So, it's just a wastage of memory space

3.2   Stack using Linked List

A stack is a last in first out and all the operations Pop, Push, Peek, and Display
can be performed with the help of a top variable. In the stack Implementation, a
stack contains a top pointer. which is the Head of the stack where pushing and
popping items happens at the head of the list. The first node has a null in the link
field and second node-link has the first node address in the link field and so on and
the last node address is in the "top" pointer. Here Push operation is accomplished
by inserting a new node at the top or start of the list. Pop is done by removing
the element from the top of the list.

The main advantage of using a linked list over arrays is that it is possible to
implement a stack that can shrink or grow as much as needed. Using an array will
put a restriction on the maximum capacity of the array which can lead to stack
overflow. Here each new node will be dynamically allocated, so overflow is not
possible.

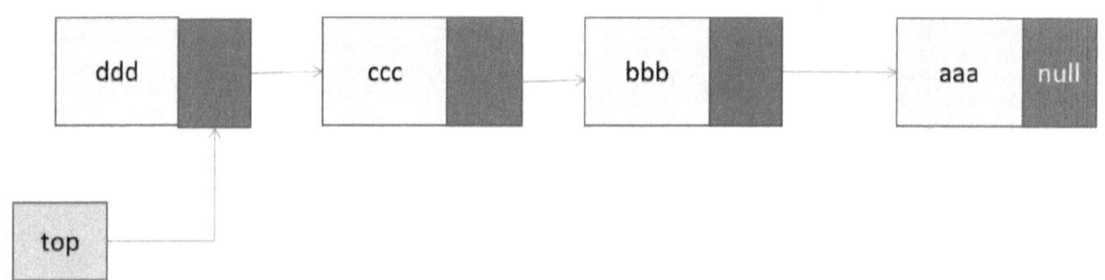

Figure 3.21: Stack using Linked List

Stack Operations:

- push(): Insert a new element into the stack
    i.e just insert a new element at the beginning of the linked list.

- pop(): Return the top element of the Stack
    i.e simply delete the first element from the linked list.

- peek(): Return the top element.

- display(): Print all elements in Stack.

Push Operation

Inserting a node to the top of stack is referred to as PUSH operation. It is similar
to adding a node at the front of the linked list.
Create a node first and allocate memory to it.
If the list is empty then the item is to be pushed as the start node of the list.
This includes assigning value to the data part of the node and assign null to the

address part of the node.

If there are some nodes in the list already, then we have to add the new element in the beginning of the list (to not violate the property of the stack). For this purpose, assign the address of the starting element to the address field of the new node and make the new node, the starting node of the list.

Algorithm: PUSH(item)

```
 1. new=getnode(AVAIL)
 2. If (new=NULL)
 3.        print "Memory underflow"
 4. else
 5.          new->data= ITEM
 6.           new->link=null
 7.           if (Top=null)
 8.                  Top= new
 9.             else
10.             new->link=Top
11.              Top=new
             [End IF]
     [End IF]
12. Return
```

Pop Operation

Deleting a node from the top of stack is referred to as POP operation. It is similar to removing a node from front of the linked list.

First Check whether there is any node present in the Stack(Check for the underflow condition).The stack will be empty if the head pointer of the list points to null. If no element then return.

Otherwise make pointer, say temp to the top node and move forward the top node and free this temp node. The next node of the head node now becomes the head node.

Algorithm: POP

```
 1. If Top= null
 2.             print " Stack Empty "
 3. Else
 4.           Set ITEM = Top-> data
 5.           Set ptr = Top
 6.           Set Top = ptr-> link
 7.           Free ptr
    [end if]
 8. Return ITEM
```

Peep Operation

Checking id stack is empty or not an Printing the top element is stack is not empty is referred to as PEEP operation.
Check if there is any node present or not, if no element then return. Otherwise print /return the value of top node of the linked list.

Algorithm: PEEP

```
1. If Top= null
2.          print " Stack Empty "
3. Else
4.           Set ITEM = Top-> data
5.           Return ITEM
   [end if]
```

Display Operation

Take a temp node and initialize it with top pointer. Move the temporary pointer through all the nodes of the list and print the value field attached to every node until it encounters NULL.

Algorithm: DISPLAY

```
1. If Top= null
2.          print " Stack Empty "
3. Else
4.   Set ptr = Top
5. Repeat Step 6-8 till ptr!=NULL
6.           Set ITEM = ptr-> data
7.           Print ITEM
8.           Set ptr = ptr-> link
     [end if]
9. Return
```

3.3   Queue using Linked List

A queue is a first in first out (FIFO) Data Structure. The queue which is implemented using a linked list can work for the variable size of data. For a queue, the last inserted node is always pointed by 'rear' and the first node is always pointed by 'front'.
In the linked queue, there are two pointers maintained in the memory i.e. front pointer and rear pointer. The front pointer contains the address of the starting element of the queue while the rear pointer contains the address of the last element of the queue.

Insertion and deletions are performed at rear and front end respectively. If front and rear both are NULL, it indicates that the queue is empty. The linked representation of queue is shown in the following figure.

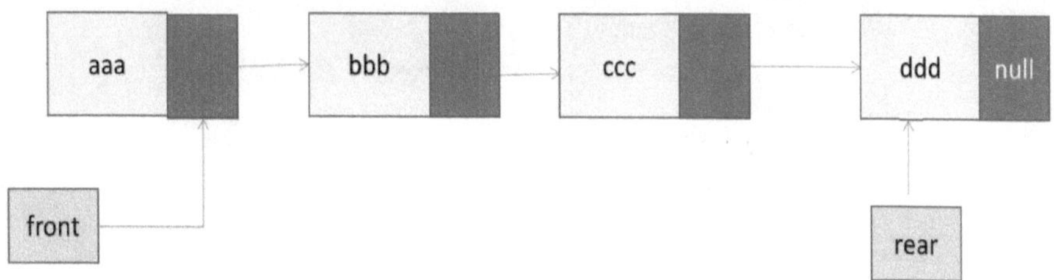

Figure 3.22: Queue using Linked List

The main advantage of using a linked list over arrays is that it is possible to implement a queue that can shrink or grow as much as needed. Using an array will put a restriction on the maximum capacity of the array which can lead to queue overflow. Here each new node will be dynamically allocated, so overflow is not possible.

Queue Operations:

- enQueue():
    This operation adds a new node after the rear and moves the rear to the next node.

- deQueue():
    This operation removes the front node and moves the front to the next node.

- display(): Print all elements in Queue.

Enqueue Operation

Insert operation or insertion on a linked queue adds an element to the end of the queue. $O(1)$ time is required. The new element which is added becomes the last element of the queue. The Rear or last pointer can be used to follow the last item.

First, build a new node with given data.
Check if the queue is empty or not.
If a queue is empty then, a new node is assigned to the front and rear.
Else make next of rear as new node and rear as a new node.

Algorithm: Enqueue(ITEM)

```
1. new=GetNode(AVAIL)
2. If (new=NULL)
```

```
  3.        print "Memory underflow"
  4. else
  5.            new->data= ITEM
  6.           new->link=null
  7.           if (Front=null)
  8.                 Front=new, Rear=new
  9.            else
 10.            Rear->link=new
 11.            Rear=new
              [End IF]
        [End IF]
 12. Return
```

Dequeue Operation

Deletion or delete operation on a linked queue removes the element which was first inserted in the queue, i.e., always the first element of the queue is removed. The first element of the queue is always removed by the dequeue function. O(1) time is required. There must be at least one element in the queue for dequeue; else, underflow situations would arise.

Check if the queue is empty or not. If queue empty, then dequeue is not possible.
Else store front in temp. And make the next of front as the front.
Delete temp, i.e, free(temp).

Algorithm: Dequeue

```
 1. If Front= null
 2.              print " Queue Empty "
 3. Else
 4.            Set ITEM = Front-> data
 5.            Set ptr = Front
 6.            Set Front = ptr-> link
 7.            Free ptr
    [end if]
 8. Return ITEM
```

Display Operation

The queue's content is shown using the print function. The print function's time complexity is O(n), where n is the number of nodes in the queue, because we must iterate through each element of the queue in order to print it.
Check if queue contains at least one element or not.
If the queue is empty print "No elements in the queue."
Else, define a node pointer and initialize it with the front.

Display data of node pointer until the next node pointer becomes NULL.

Algorithm: Display

```
1. If (Front= null)
2.              print " Queue Empty "
3. Else
4.   Set ptr = Front
5. Repeat Step 6-8 till ptr!=NULL
6.              Set ITEM = ptr-> data
7.              Print ITEM
8.              Set ptr = ptr-> link
      [end if]
9. Return
```

3.4   Polynomial Representation Using Linked List

A polynomial is composed of different terms where each of them holds a coefficient and an exponent. A polynomial is a sum of terms where each term has the form ax^e , where x is the variable, a is the coefficient and e is the exponent.

A polynomial p(x) is the expression in variable x which is in the form $a_n x^n + a_{n-1} x^{n-1} + \cdots + a_1 x + a_0$ where $a_n, a_{n-1}, \cdots, a_1, a_0$ falls in the category of real numbers and 'n' is non negative integer, which is called the degree of polynomial. We will assume an ordering of the terms in the polynomial such that $e_n > e_{n-1} > ... > e_2 > e_1 \geq 0$.

A polynomial expression is represented as nodes which consists of three fields: one is the coefficient (COEFF), other is the exponent (EXP) and link that points to the next node (LINK).

Example: $3x^8 - 7x^6 + 14x^3 + 10x - 5$, would be stored as shown in Figure

Figure 3.23: Linked list representation of a polynomial in single variable

The terms whose coefficients are zero are not stored.

Polynomial addition

In order to add two polynomials, say P and Q, to get a resultant polynomial R, we have to compare their terms starting at their first nodes and moving towards the end one by one. There may arise three cases during the comparison between the terms of two polynomials.

Case 1: The exponents of two terms are equal. Here, the coefficients in the two nodes are added and a new term is created with the values

Rptr− >COEFF = Pptr− >COEFF +Qptr− >COEFF

Rptr− >EXP = Pptr− >EXP

Case 2: Pptr− >EXP > Qptr− >EXP, ie. The exponent of the current term in P is greater than the exponent of the current term in Q. Then, a duplicate of the current term in P is created and inserted in the polynomial R.

Case 3: Pptr− >EXP < Qptr− > EXP ie. the case when the exponent of the current term in P is less than the exponent of the current term in Q. Here, a duplicate of the current term of Q is created and inserted in the polynomial R.

Algorithm: PolynomialAdd_LL
Input: Two polynomials P and Q with PSTART and QSTART.
Output: A polynomial R is the sum of P and Q with RSTART as NULL.
Data structure: Single linked list structure for representing a term in a single variable polynomial

```
Pptr = PSTART, Qptr = QSTART
While  (Pptr != NULL) and (Qptr!=NULL) do
    CASE:Pptr->EXP = Qptr->EXP        //Case 1
            AddNode( Pptr->COEFF + Qptr->COEFF,Pptr->EXP)
            Pptr = Pptr->LINK, Qptr = Qptr->LINK
    CASE:Pptr->EXP > Qptr->EXP        //Case 2
            AddNode( Pptr->COEFF,Pptr->EXP)
            Pptr = Pptr->LINK
    CASE:Pptr->EXP < QPTR->EXP        //Case 3
            AddNode( Qptr->COEFF,Qptr->EXP)
            Qptr = Qptr->LINK
EndWhile

if(Pptr!=NULL) and (Qptr = NULL) then
   While (Pptr!=NULL) do
     AddNode( Pptr->COEFF,Pptr->EXP)
     Pptr = Pptr->LINK
   EndWhile
Endif
```

```
if (Pptr = NULL) and (Qptr!=NULL) then
    While ()Qptr != NULL) do
        AddNode( Qptr->COEFF,Qptr->EXP)
        Qptr = Qptr->LINK
    EndWhile
Endif
```

AddNode is a function to create a polynomial linked list with RSTART. Same algorithm as create linked list.

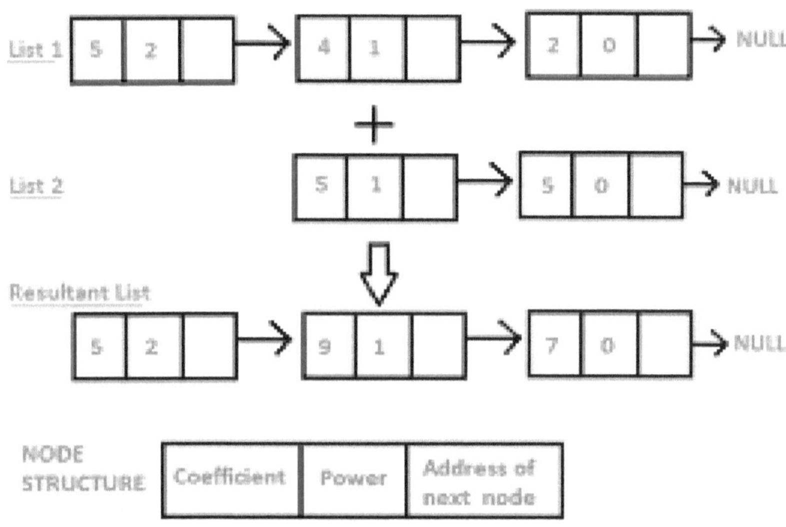

Figure 3.24: Polynomial addition

Polynomial Multiplication

Here two polynomials P and Q are considered to be multiplied and the result will be stored in another polynomial R. The method is quite straightforward: Let Pptr denote the current term in P and Qptr be that of in Q. For each term of P we have to visit all the terms in Q: the exponent values in two terms are added (R− >EXP = P− >EXP + Q− > EXP), the coefficient values are multiplied (R− >COEFF = P− >COEFF * Q− >COEFF), and these values are included into R in such a way that if there is no term in R whose exponent value is the same as the exponent value obtained by adding the exponents from P and Q, then create a new node and insert it to R with the values so obtained (that is, R− >COEFF and R− >EXP); on the other hand, if a node is found in R having same exponent value R− >EXP, then update the coefficient value of it by adding the resultant coefficient(R− >COEFF) in it.

Algorithm PolynomialMultiply_LL

Input: Two polynomials P and Q having their headers as PHEADER, QHEADER.
output: A polynomial R storing the result of multiplication of P and Q
Data Structure: Single linked list structure for representing a term in a single variable polynomial.

```
Pptr = PSTART, Qptr = QSTART

if(Pptr->LINK = NULL) or (Qptr->LINK = NULL) then
    EXIT
EndIf
Pptr = Pptr->LINK
While (Pptr!=NULL) do
    While (Qptr!=NULL) do
        C = Pptr->COEFF x Qptr->COEFF
        X = Ppt->EXP + Qptr->EXP

        /search for the equal exponent value in R/

        Rptr = RSTART
        While(Rptr!=NULL) and (Rptr->EXP>X) do
            Rptr1=Rptr
            Rptr=Rptr->LINK
            if(Rptr->EXP = X) then
                Rpt->COEFF = Rptr->COEFF + C
            Else
                new=GetNode(NODE)
                new->EXP = X, new->COEFF = C
            If(Rptr->LINK = NULL) then
                Rptr->LINK = new
                new->LINK = NULL
            Else
                Rptr1->LINK = new
                new->LINK = Rptr
            Endif
        Endif
    EndWhile
EndWhile

Stop
```

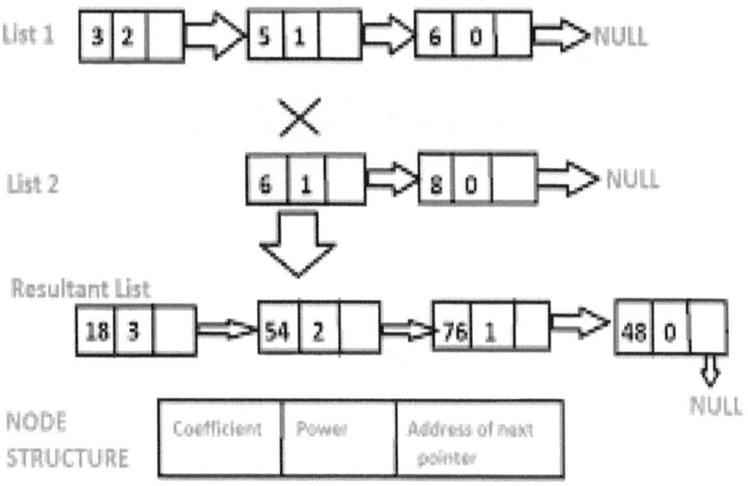

Figure 3.25: Polynomial Multiplication

Polynomials having multiple variables

Till now we have considered the case of a polynomial of a single variable. The idea now can be extended to represent any polynomial with two variables, three variables, and so on. Below is a structure of a node that will be suitable to represent a polynomial with three variables x, y and z using a single linked list.

COEFF	EXPX	EXPY	EXPZ	LINK

Figure 3.26: Polynomial with 3 variables node structure

Writing procedures to manipulate such polynomials is as simple as the earlier procedures for polynomials with single variables. These are left as an assignment to the reader.

3.5 Memory Management

The basic task of any program is to manipulate data. These data should be stored in memory during their manipulation. The basic model for memory management is that we have a (large) block of contiguous memory locations, which we will call the **memory pool**. Periodically, memory requests are issued for some amount of space in the pool. A memory manager has the job of finding a contiguous block of locations of at least the requested size from somewhere within the memory pool.

Honoring such a request is called **memory allocation**. At some point, space that has been requested might no longer be needed, and this space can be returned to the memory manager so that it can be reused. This is called a **memory deallocation**.

There are two memory management schemes for the storage allocations of data:

1. Static storage management
2. Dynamic storage management

Static Memory allocation

Static memory allocation is also known as Compile-time memory allocation because the memory is allocated during compile time. In this type of memory allocation, the memory that the program can use is fixed i.e. we cannot allocate or deallocate memory during the program's execution. In many applications, it is not possible to predict how much memory will be needed by the program at run time.

Example: int x, y; float a[5];

When the first statement is encountered, the compiler will allocate two bytes to each variables x and y. The second statement results into the allocation of 20 bytes to the array a (5*4, where there are five elements and each element of float type tales four bytes).

Properties of Static Memory allocation

- Memory allocation is done during compile time.

- Stack Memory is used here.

- Memory cannot be changed while executing a program.

- The static memory allocation is fast and saves running time.

- It is less efficient as compared to Dynamic memory allocation.

- The allocation process is simple and easy to use.

Disadvantages of Static Memory allocation

- This allocation method leads to memory wastage.

- Memory cannot be changed while executing a program.

- Exact memory requirements must be known.

- If memory is not required, it cannot be freed.

Dynamic Memory allocation

Dynamic memory allocation is also known as Runtime memory allocation because the memory is allocated during runtime or program execution. The allocation and release of the memory space can be done using the library functions of stdlib.h header file. These functions allocate memory from a memory area called heap and deallocate this memory whenever not required so that it can be used for some other purpose.

Sl. No	Static Memory Allocation	Dynamic Memory Allocation
1	In the static memory allocation, variables get allocated permanently, till the program executes or function call finishes.	In the Dynamic memory allocation, variables get allocated only if your program unit gets active.
2	Static Memory Allocation is done before program execution.	Dynamic Memory Allocation is done during program execution.
3	It uses stack for managing the static allocation of memory	It uses heap for managing the dynamic allocation of memory
4	It is less efficient	It is more efficient
5	In Static Memory Allocation, there is no memory re-usability	In Dynamic Memory Allocation, there is memory re-usability and memory can be freed when not required
6	In static memory allocation, once the memory is allocated, the memory size can not change.	In dynamic memory allocation, when memory is allocated the memory size can be changed.
7	In this memory allocation scheme, we cannot reuse the unused memory.	This allows reusing the memory. The user can allocate more memory when required. Also, the user can release the memory when the user needs it.
8	In this memory allocation scheme, execution is faster than dynamic memory allocation.	In this memory allocation scheme, execution is slower than static memory allocation.
9	In this memory is allocated at compile time.	In this memory is allocated at run time.
10	In this allocated memory remains from start to end of the program.	In this allocated memory can be released at any time during the program.
11	Example: This static memory allocation is generally used for array.	Example: This dynamic memory allocation is generally used for linked list.

Functions calloc() and malloc() support allocating dynamic memory. In the Dynamic allocation of memory space is allocated by using these functions when the value is returned by functions and assigned to pointer variables.

There are various principles on which the dynamic memory management scheme is based. These principles are listed below.

1. Allocation Schemes: Here, we discuss how a request for a memory block will be serviced. There are two strategies:

   (a) Fixed Block Allocation
   (b) Variable Block Allocation: There are 4 strategies
      - First Fit.
      - Next Fit
      - Best Fit
      - Worst Fit

2. Deallocation Schemes: Here, we discuss how to return a memory block to the memory bank whenever it is no longer required. Two strategies are:

   (a) Random Deallocation
   (b) Ordered Deallocation

Memory Representation A memory bank or a pool of free storages is often a collection of non-contiguous blocks of memory. Their linearity can be maintained by means of pointers between one block to another, or in other words a memory bank is a linked list where links maintain the adjacency of blocks. Regarding the size of the blocks, there are two practices: fixed block storage and variable block storage.

3.5.1 Fixed Block Storage

This is the simplest storage maintenance method. Here each block is of the same size. The size is determined by the system manager (user). Here, the memory manager (a program of OS) maintains a pointer AVAIL which points a list of non-contiguous memory blocks. The below figure shows a memory bank with fixed size blocks.

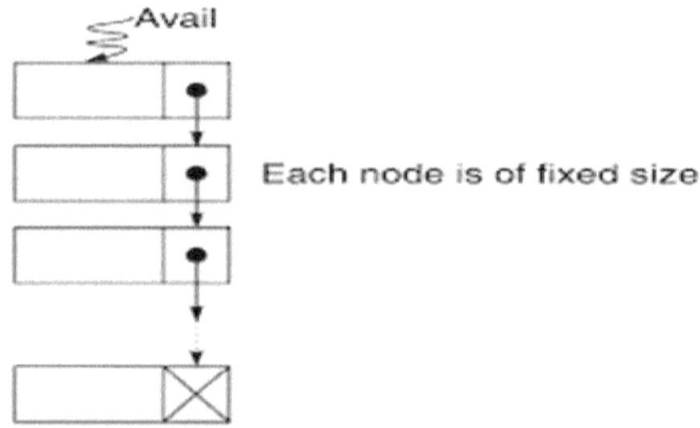

Figure 3.27: Pool of free storage with fixed size blocks

A user communicates with the memory manager by means of two functions GetNode and ReturnNode()

Algorithm: GetNode

Input: This procedure avails a block from memory bank for a datatype represented by NODE

*Output:*Returns a pointer to the memory block is available else NULL

```
Steps
1.If (AVAIL = NULL) then                    // memory exhausted
2.       Print "Memory Insufficient"
3.Else
4.      ptr= AVAIL
5.      AVAIL= AVAIL->LINK
6.  Return ptr      // return ptr of available block to caller
    [end if]
```

The procedure GetNode is to get a memory block to store data of type Node. It returns a pointer to the first block in the pool of free storage. The AVAIL then points to the next block. The link modification is shown in figure. If AVAIL =NULL, it indicates that no more memory is available for allocation.

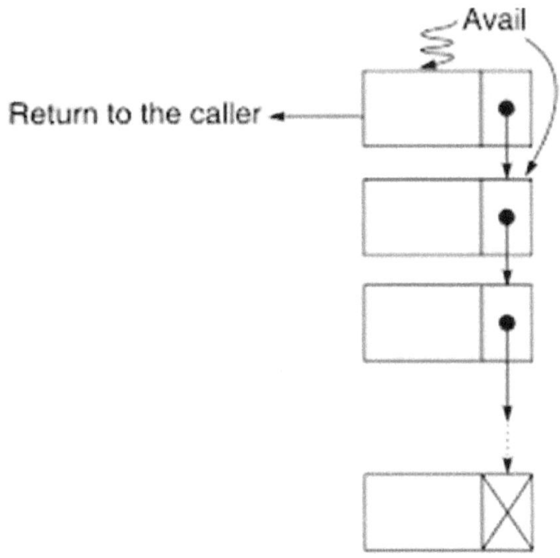

Figure 3.28: Getting a block from the memory bank

Similarly, whenever a memory block is no more required, it can be returned to the memory bank through a procedure ReturnNode :

Algorithm: ReturnNode

Input: This procedure returns a block from memory referenced by PTR
Output: The memory block is returned to the memory bank.


```
Steps
1. ptr1= AVAIL
2. while( ptr1->LINK != NULL) Repeat Step 3
3.        ptr1= ptr1->LINK         // traverse to end of AVAIL list
   [end while]
4.        ptr1->LINK= PTR
5.       PTR->LINK=NULL
6.   Return
```

ReturnNode appends the returned block (PTR) to the end of the free storage
pool or memory pool AVAIL. The memory pool is traversed till the end and then
memory block pointed by PTR is appended to the pool. Change in pointers is as
shown in figure.

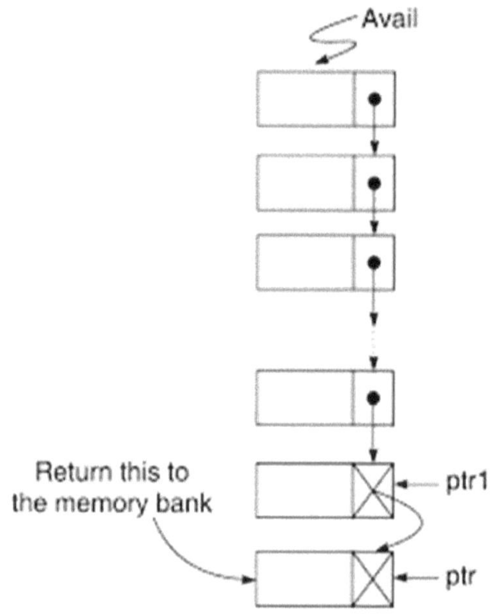

Figure 3.29: Returing a block to the memory bank

Advantages of Fixed Block Storage:
Simple to implement.
Easy to manage and design.

Disadvantages of Fixed Block Storage:
This scheme suffers from internal fragmentation.
The size of block is specified at the time of system generation.
Making the size of block larger causes internal Fragmentation and making the size
of block too small reduces space wastage bur reduces the overall performance.

Variable Block Allocation

This scheme of maintaining variable size of blocks in memory overcomes the disadvantages of fixed block storage. Here, whenever a request for memory comes, GetNode procedure will return a block of memory exactly of the same size or more than the size that the use program request to the memory manager. ReturnNode will dispose a block into the free storage pool whenever the program returns back the memory block when not required.

Example:
Consider a system where initially no programs are running, as in Figure (a). The whole memory space is available.

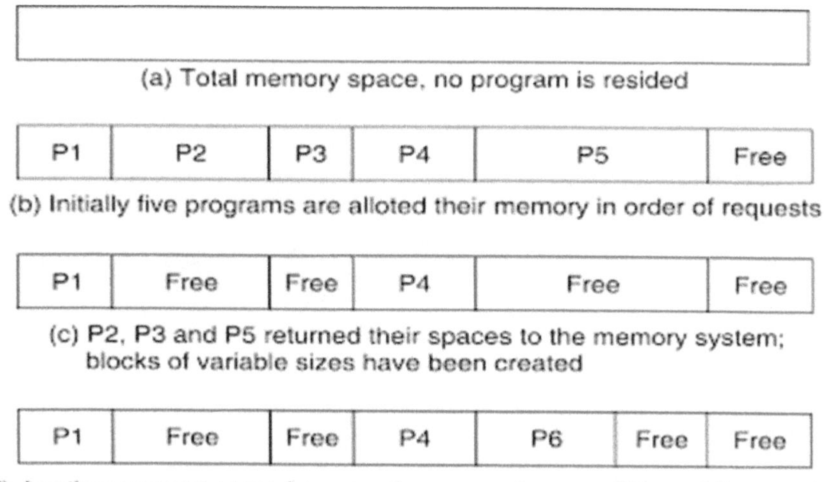

Figure 3.30: Partitioning memory into smaller blocks for dynamic memory Allocation

In Figure (b) , 5 processes have been allocated in order of their requests. At a later stage processes P2, P3 and P5 gets over and their memory has been returned back to memory pool as shown in Figure (c). Figure (d) shows how the free space has been split into smaller block for process P6.

3.5.2   Variable Block Storage Allocation Strategies

Memory allocations are made through variations on the familiar malloc( ) call.
Basically can be defined as

1. Traverse the tree to find the block to fit the request.

2. If the size of the block found is equal or greater than to the requested size,
   return the block.

3. If the found is block that is much larger, then split it into an allocated block
   and unallocated block and return the free block back to pool.

4. If we didn't find any block at least as large as the request, then return
   memory allocation failed and wait for free memory space.

There are different Allocation schemes in variable Block Allocation.

1. First Fit Algorithm

   First Fit algorithm scans the linked list and whenever it finds the first big
   enough hole to store a process, it stops scanning and load the process into
   that hole. This procedure produces two partitions. Out of them, one partition will be a hole while the other partition will store the process.

   First Fit algorithm maintains the linked list according to the increasing order
   of starting index. This is the simplest to implement among all the algorithms
   and produces bigger holes as compare to the other algorithms.

2. Next Fit Algorithm

   Next Fit algorithm is similar to First Fit algorithm except the fact that,
   Next fit scans the linked list from the node where it previously allocated a
   hole.

   Next fit doesn't scan the whole list, it starts scanning the list from the next
   node. The idea behind the next fit is the fact that the list has been scanned
   once therefore the probability of finding the hole is larger in the remaining
   part of the list.

   Experiments over the algorithm have shown that the next fit is not better
   than the first fit. So, it is not being used these days in most of the cases.

3. Best Fit Algorithm

   The Best Fit algorithm tries to find out the smallest hole possible in the list
   that can accommodate the size requirement of the process.

   Using Best Fit has some disadvantages.

   - It is slower because it scans the entire list every time and tries to find
     out the smallest hole which can satisfy the requirement the process.

- Due to the fact that the difference between the whole size and the process size is very small, the holes produced will be as small as it cannot be used to load any process and therefore it remains useless. [Internal Fragmentation]

Despite of the fact that the name of the algorithm is best fit, It is not the best algorithm among all.

4. Worst Fit Algorithm

The worst fit algorithm scans the entire list every time and tries to find out the biggest hole in the list which can fulfill the requirement of the process.

Despite of the fact that this algorithm produces the larger holes to load the other processes, this is not the better approach due to the fact that it is slower because it searches the entire list every time again and again.

Example 1:

Consider six memory partitions of size 200 KB, 400 KB, 600 KB, 500 KB, 300 KB and 250 KB. These partitions need to be allocated to four processes of sizes 357 KB, 210 KB, 468 KB and 491 KB in that order. Perform the allocation of processes using-First Fit Algorithm, Best Fit Algorithm, Worst Fit Algorithm.

The main memory has been divided into fixed size partitions as-

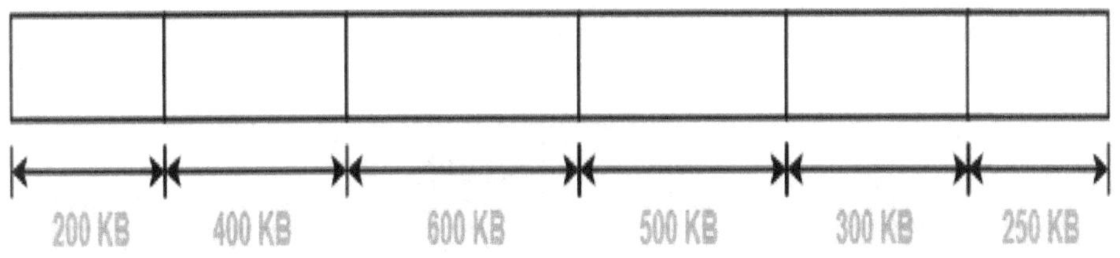

Main Memory

Given processes are-
Process P1 = 357 KB
Process P2 = 210 KB
Process P3 = 468 KB
Process P4 = 491 KB

In **First Fit Algorithm,**

* Algorithm starts scanning the partitions serially.

* When a partition big enough to store the process is found, it allocates that partition to the process.

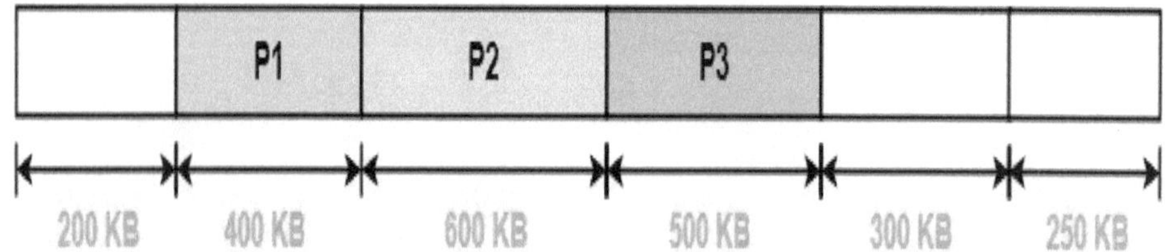

Main Memory

When P1 is allocated the is a free space of 43 Kb (400KB-357KB).
When P2 is allocated the is a free space of 390 Kb (600KB-210KB).
When P1 is allocated the is a free space of 32 Kb (500KB-468KB).
The free space is returned back to pool and may be utilized if required too.

Process P4 cannot be allocated the memory. This is because no partition of size 491 that fits, which may be greater than or equal to the size of process P4 is available.

In **Best Fit Algorithm,**

* Algorithm first scans all the partitions.

* It then allocates the partition of smallest size that can store the process.

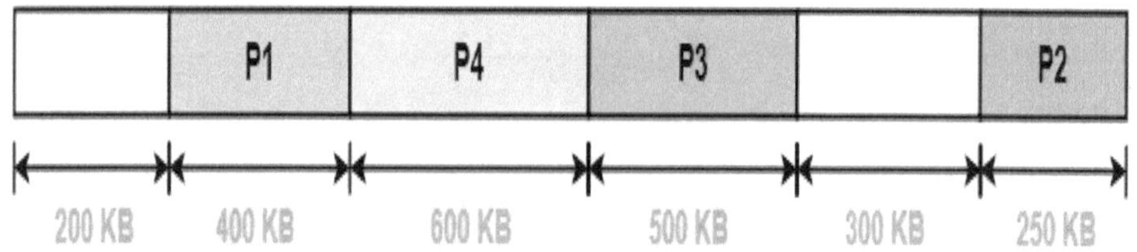

Main Memory

Here as the whole list of free blocks are searched, to find a hole big enough, that is smallest among all holes, P2 gets allocated in block of 250KB and hence 600 KB can be used for allocating P4.

In **Worst Fit Algorithm,**

* Algorithm first scans all the partitions.

* It then allocates the partition of largest size to the process.

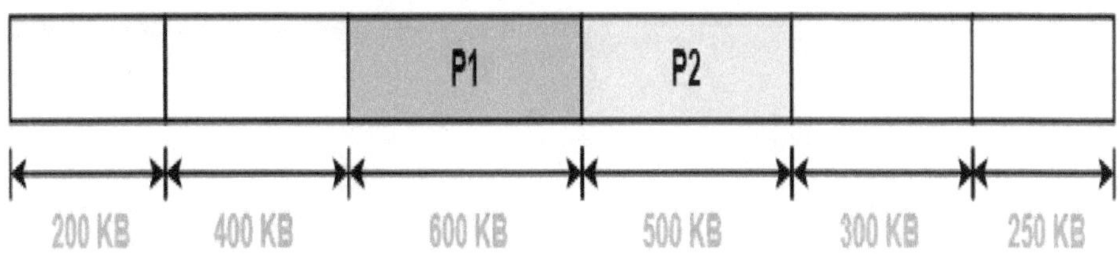

Main Memory

Process P3 and Process P4 cannot be allocated the memory. This is because no partition of size greater than or equal to the size of process P3 and process P4 is available.

Example 2: Given memory partitions of 100K, 500K, 200K, 300K, and 600K (in order), how would each of the First-fit, Best-fit, and Worst-fit algorithms place processes of 212K, 417K, 112K, and 426K (in order)? Which algorithm makes the most efficient use of memory?

Solution:

First-Fit:
212K is put in 500K partition.
417K is put in 600K partition.
112K is put in 288K partition (new partition 288K = 500K - 212K).
426K must wait.

Best-Fit:
212K is put in 300K partition.
417K is put in 500K partition.
112K is put in 200K partition.
426K is put in 600K partition.

Worst-Fit:
212K is put in 600K partition.
417K is put in 500K partition.
112K is put in 388K partition.
426K must wait.

In this example, Best-Fit turns out to be the best.

Module 4

4.1 Trees

Arrays, linked lists, stacks and queues were examples of linear data structures in which elements are arranged in a linear fashion (ie, one dimensional representation). Tree is another very useful data structure in which elements are appearing in a non-linear fashion, which requires a two-dimensional representation.

A tree is a nonlinear abstract data type with a hierarchy-based structure. It consists of nodes (where the data is stored) that are connected via links. The tree data structure stems from a single node called a root node and has subtrees connected to the root.

4.1.1   Tree Terminologies

* Node: A node is an entity that contains a key or value and pointers to its child nodes.
* Edge : It is the link between any two nodes.
* Path :Path refers to the sequence of nodes along the edges of a tree.
* Root : The node at the top of the tree is called root. There is only one root per tree and one path from the root node to any node.
* Parent: Any node except the root node has one edge upward to a node called parent.
* Child : The node below a given node connected by its edge downward is called its child node.
* Leaf : The node which does not have any child node is called the leaf node or external node. The node having at least a child node is called an internal node.
* Subtree : Subtree represents the descendants of a node.
* Visiting : Visiting refers to checking the value of a node when control is on the node.

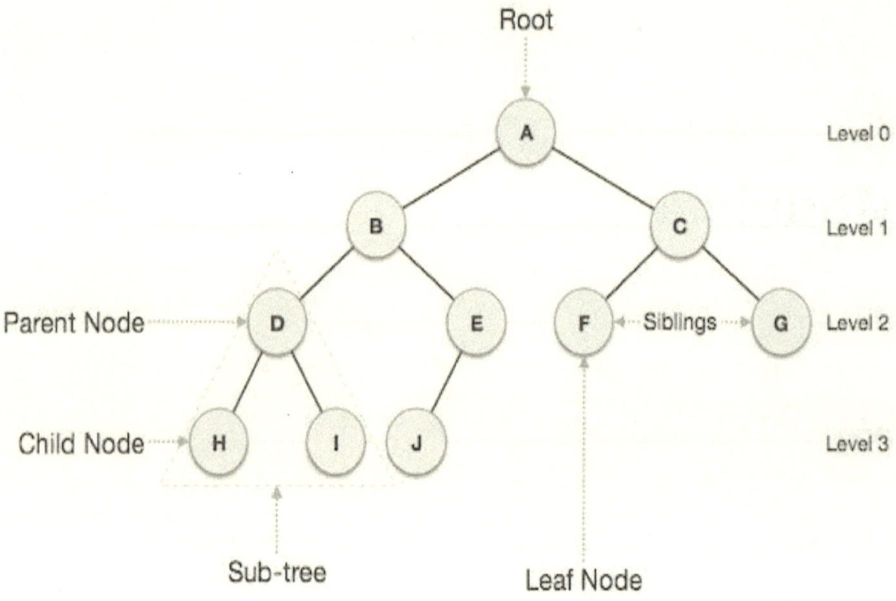

Figure 4.1: Tree as a Data Structure

* Traversing : Traversing means passing through nodes in a specific order.

* Levels : Level of a node represents the generation of a node. If the root node is at level 0, then its next child node is at level 1, its grandchild is at level 2, and so on.

* Keys : Key represents a value of a node based on which a search operation is to be carried out for a node.

* Height of a Node: The height of a node is the number of edges from the node to the deepest leaf (ie. the longest path from the node to a leaf node).

* Depth of a Node: The depth of a node is the number of edges from the root to the node.

* Height of a Tree :The height of a Tree is the height of the root node or the depth of the deepest node.

* Degree of a Node: In the tree data structure, the total number of children of a node is called the degree of the node. The highest degree of the node among all the nodes in a tree is called the Degree of Tree.

There are three types of trees :

- General Trees

- Binary Trees

- Binary Search Trees

General Trees General trees are unordered tree data structures where the root node has minimum 0 or maximum 'n' subtrees. The General trees have no constraint placed on their hierarchy. The root node thus acts like the superset of all the other subtrees.

Recursive Definition: A tree is a finite set of one or more nodes such that:
(i) there is a specially designated node called as the root.
(ii) the remaining nodes are partitioned into n (n>0) disjoint sets $T_1, T_2, ...T_n$, where each T_i(i=1,2,3...n) is a tree. $T_1, T_2, ...T_n$, are called subtrees of the root.

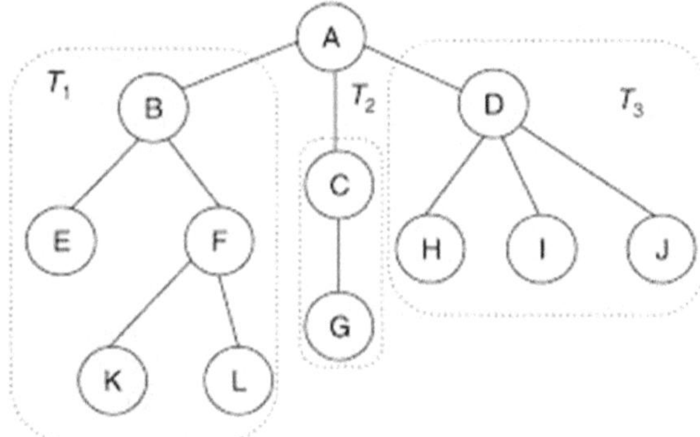

4.1.2   Binary Trees

Binary Trees are general trees in which the root node can only hold up to maximum 2 subtrees: left subtree and right subtree.

Recursive Definition: A binary tree is a finite set of nodes such that:
(i) T can be empty(called empty binary tree) or
(ii) There is a specially designated node called as the root of T, and the reaming nodes of T form two disjoint binary treesT_1 and T_2whihc are called the left and right subtree respectively.

Binary trees are divided into three types.

-Full Binary Tree : A full binary tree is a binary tree type where every node has either 0 or 2 child nodes.

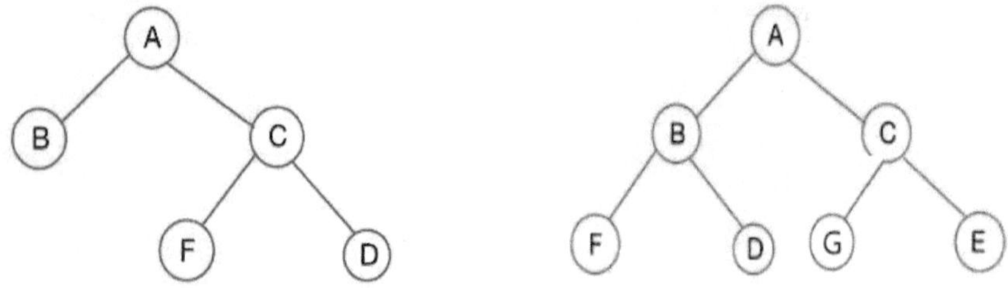

Figure 4.2: Full Binary Tree

-Complete Binary Tree: A binary tree is said to be a complete binary tree if all its levels, except possibly the last level, have the maximum number of possible nodes, and all the nodes in the last level appear as far left as possible.

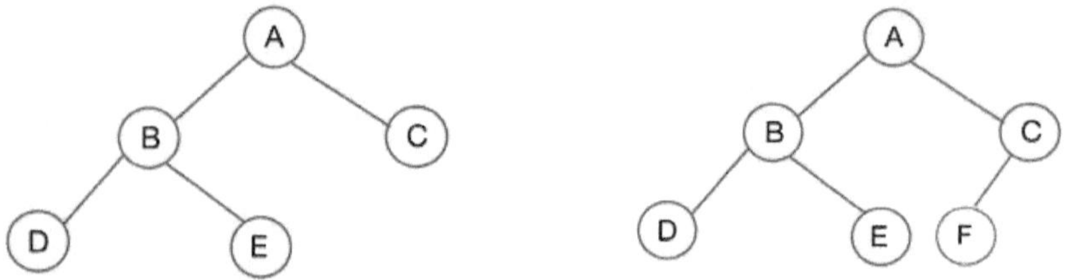

Figure 4.3: Complete Binary Tree

-Perfect Binary Tree: A perfect binary tree is a binary tree type where all the leaf nodes are on the same level and every node except leaf nodes have 2 children.

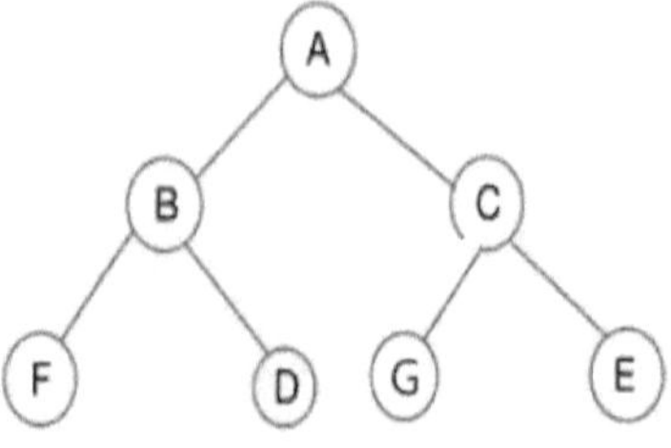

Figure 4.4: Perfect Binary Tree

Binary Search Trees Binary Search Trees possess all the properties of Binary Trees including some extra properties of their own, based on some constraints, making them more efficient than binary trees.

The data in the Binary Search Trees (BST) is always stored in such a way that the values in the left subtree are always less than the values in the root node and the values in the right subtree are always greater than the values in the root node, i.e. left subtree < root node < right subtree.

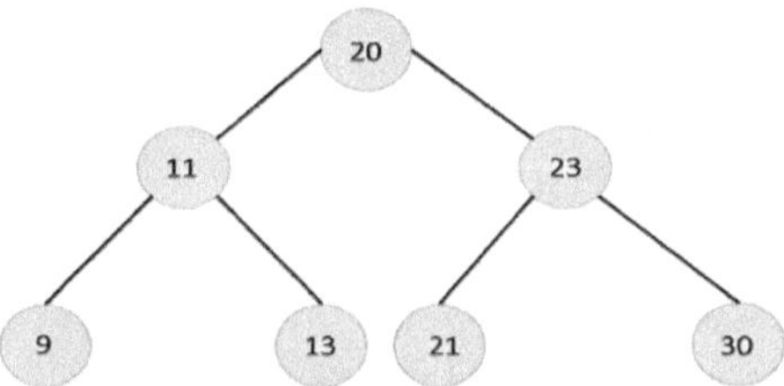

Binary Search Tree Data Structure

Figure 4.5: Binary Search Tree

4.1.3 Representations of Binary Tree

Sequential / Linear representation using arrays

The array representation of binary tree can be done using a technique called level order traversal. In level-order traversal, the elements of the binary tree are stored in the array in the order in which they are visited in a breadth-first search.

The array representation of binary tree allows for efficient access to the elements of the tree. For example, if a binary tree has n nodes, the array representation of the tree can be stored in an array of size n, allowing for constant-time access to each node in the tree.

In this representation, the root node of the binary tree is stored at the first position of the array, and its left and right children are stored at the second and third positions, respectively. The remaining nodes are stored in the same way, with the children of each node stored in consecutive positions in the array.
For any node with index I

$$LCHILD(i) = 2 * I$$
$$RCHILD(i) = (2 * i) + 1$$
$$PARENT(i) = i/2,$$

For the node when i=1, there is no parent. If $2* i > n$, then i has no child

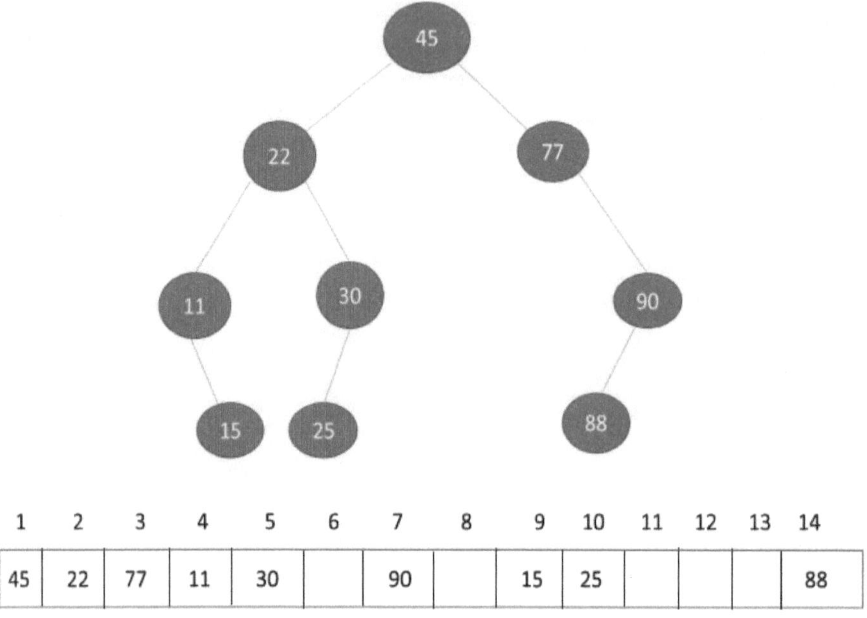

Figure 4.6: Array representation of a Binary Tree

Advantages Sequential representation-:

1. Any node can be accessed from any other node by calculating the index.

2. Here, data is stored simply without any pointers to their successor or predecessor. But can be accessed by index value

3. Programming languages, where dynamic memory allocation is not possible (like BASIC, FORTRAN), array representation is only possible.

Disadvantages Sequential representation-:

1. Other than full binary trees, majority of the array entries may be empty and hence space wastage.

2. It allows only static representation. It is not possible to enhance the tree structure, if the array structure is limited.

3. Inserting a new node and deletion of an existing node is difficult, because it require considerable data movement.

Linked List representation using Linked List

Binary trees in linked representation are stored in the memory as linked lists. These lists have nodes that aren't stored at adjacent or neighboring memory locations and are linked to each other through the parent-child relationship associated with trees. It consists of nodes, with Root at the top and pointers to left and right child.

Each node has three different parts –

- data element
- pointer that points towards the right node
- pointer that points towards the left node

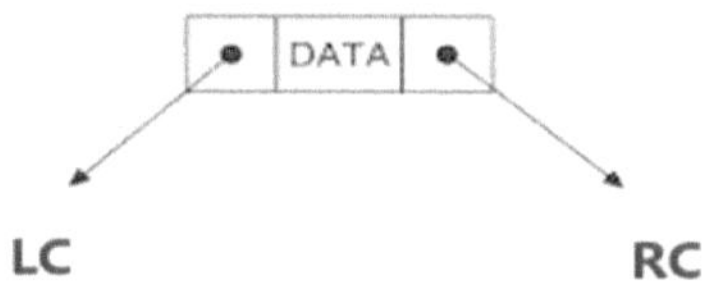

Figure 4.7: Structure of a Node

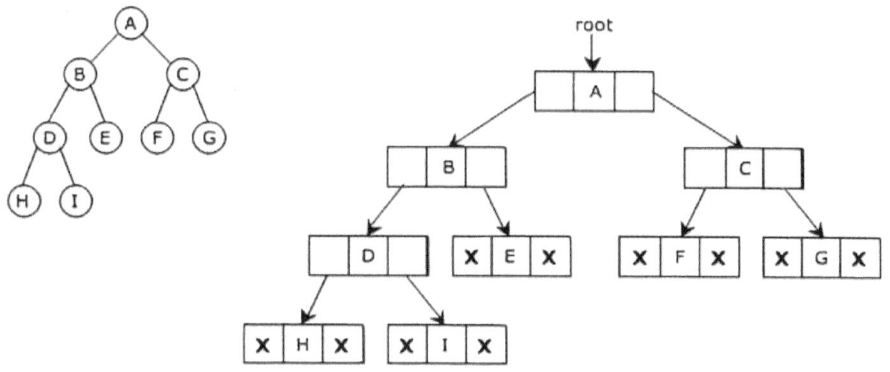

Figure 4.8: Linked List representation of Binary Search Tree

4.1.4   Tree Traversals

Traversal is a process to visit all the nodes of a tree and may print their values too. Because, all nodes are connected via edges (links) we always start from the root node. That is, we cannot random access a node in tree.

There are three ways which we use to traverse a tree –

1. Inorder traversal (T_{left}, Root, T_{right})

2. Preorder traversal (Root, T_{left}, T_{right})

3. Postorder traversal (T_{left}, T_{right}, Root)

Traversing left and right subtrees are defined recursively.

Inorder Traversal of a Binary tree

* Traverse the left sub-tree of the root node R in inorder

* Visit the root node R

* Traverse the right sub-tree of the root node R in inorder

Algorithm: Inorder

Input : ROOT is the pointer to the root node of the binary tree.
  Output : Visiting all the nodes in inorder fashion.
  Data structure : Linked structure of binary tree.

```
1. ptr = ROOT //Start from ROOT
2. if(ptr!= NULL) then       //if it is not an empty node
3. Inorder(ptr->LC)       //Traverse the left subtree of the
                               node in inorder
4. visit(ptr)            //Visit the node
5. Inorder(ptr->RC)        //Traverse the right subtree
                              of the node in inorder
   [End  if]
6.Stop
```

Preorder Traversal of a Binary tree

* Visit the root node R

* Traverse the left sub-tree of the root node R in preorder

* Traverse the right sub-tree of the root node R in preorder

Algorithm :Preorder

Input : ROOT is theroot node of the binary tree.
Output : Visiting all the nodes in preorder fashion.
*Data structure :*Linked structure of binary tree.

```
1. ptr = ROOT            //Start from ROOT
2. if(ptr!= NULL) then     //if it is not an empty node
3. visit(ptr)           //Visit the node
4. preorder(ptr->LC)      //Traverse the left subtree in preorder
5. preorder(ptr->RC)        //Traverse the right subtree in preorder
   [End if]
6. Stop
```

Postorder traversal of a binary tree

* Traverse the left sub-tree in postorder

* Traverse the right sub-tree in postorder

* Visit the root node R

Algorithm Postorder
Input : ROOT is the root node of the binary tree.
Output : Visiting all the nodes in preorder fashion.
Data structure : Linked structure of binary tree.

```
1. ptr = ROOT              //Start from ROOT
2. if(ptr!= NULL) then       //if it is not an empty node
3. postorder(ptr->LC)     //Traverse the left subtree in postorder
4. postorder(ptr->RC)        //Traverse the right subtree in postorder
5. visit(ptr)             //Visit the node
   [End if]
6. Stop
```

Algorithm Search_BST
Input : ITEM is the data to be searched.
Output : If found then pointer to the node containing data ITEM else a message.
Data structure : Linked structure of the binary tree. Pointer to the root node is
ROOT.

```
1. ptr = ROOT, flag = FALSE
2. while (ptr != NULL) and (flag=FALSE) do
3.              Case: ITEM < ptr->DATA
4.                       ptr = ptr->LCHILD
5.             Case: ptr->DATA = ITEM
6.                      flag=TRUE
7.            Case: ITEM > ptr->DATA
8.                      ptr = ptr->RCHILD
          [End Case]
     [End While]
9. if(flag = TRUE) then
10.        Print "ITEM has found at the node", ptr
11. else
12.     Print "ITEM does not exist: search is unsuccessful"
13. Return
```

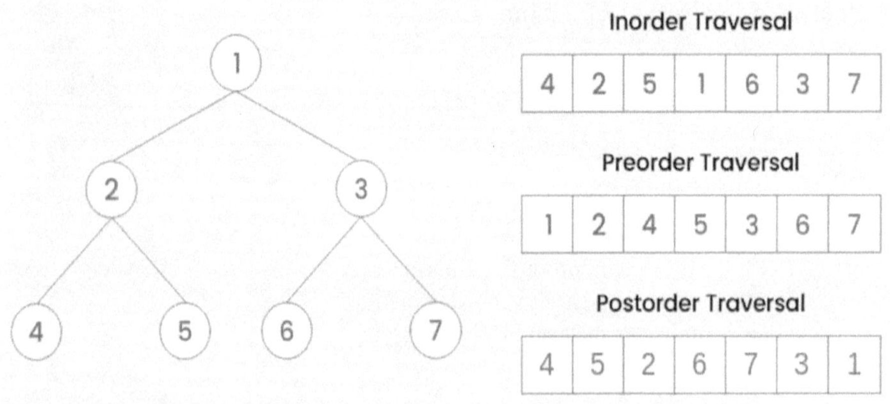

Figure 4.9: Tree Traversal Example

4.1.5 Binary Search Tree

A binary search tree follows some order to arrange the elements. In a Binary search tree, the value of left node must be smaller than the parent node, and the value of right node must be greater than the parent node. This rule is applied recursively to the left and right subtrees of the root. To arrange the data either numerical ordering or lexicographical ordering is taken.

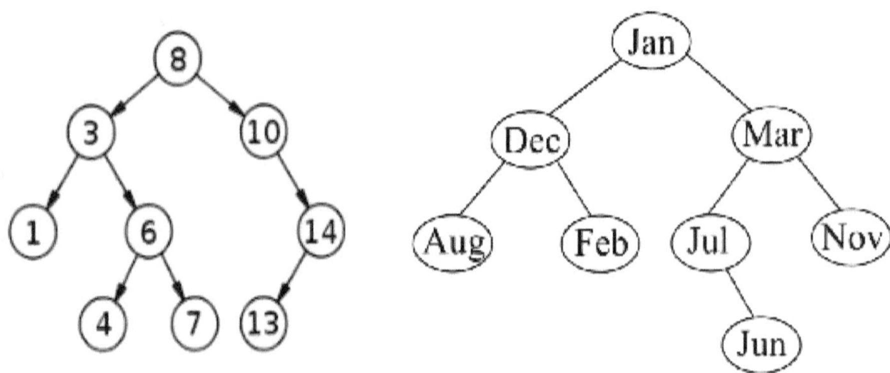

Figure 4.10: Binary Search Tree

4.1.6   Operations on Binary Search Tree

1. Searching Data
2. Inserting Data
3. Deleting Data
4. Traversing BST

Search Data in a BST

Suppose in a binary search tree T, ITEM is the element of search. We will assume that the tree is represented using a linked structure.
We start from the root node R. Then, if ITEM is less than the value in the root node R, we proceed to its left child; if ITEM is greater than the value in the node R; we proceed to its right child. The process will be continued till the item is not found or we reach a dead end, that is, the leaf node. Figure 4.12 shows the track (in shaded line) for searching of 54 in a binary search tree Repeat the above step till no more traversal is possible. If at any iteration, key is found, return True, Else False.

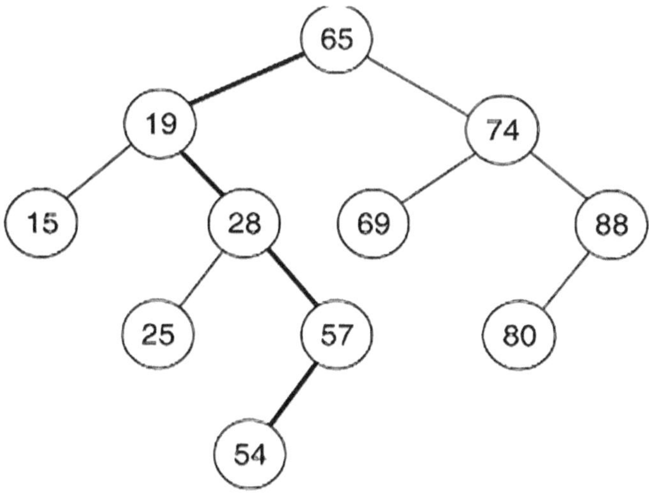

Figure 4.11: Searching 54 in a Binary Search Tree

Algorithm Search_BST

Input: ITEM is the data that has to be searched.
Output: If found then pointer to the node containing data ITEM else a message.
Data structure: Linked structure of the binary tree. Pointer to the root node is ROOT.

Steps:

1. ptr = ROOT, flag = FALSE   // Start from the root
2. **While** (ptr ≠ NULL) and (flag = FALSE) **do**
3.   **Case:** ITEM < ptr→DATA   // Go to the left sub-tree
4.   ptr = ptr→LCHILD
5.   **Case:** ptr→DATA = ITEM   // Search is successful
6.   flag = TRUE
7.   **Case:** ITEM > ptr→DATA   // Go to the right sub-tree
8.   ptr = ptr→RCHILD
9.   **EndCase**
10. **EndWhile**
11. **If** (flag = TRUE) **then**   // Search is successful
12.   **Print** "ITEM has found at the node", ptr
13. **Else**
14.   **Print** "ITEM does not exist: Search is unsuccessful"
15. **EndIf**
16. **Stop**

Insert Data in a BST

A new key is always inserted at the leaf by maintaining the property of the binary search tree. We start searching for a key from the root until we hit a leaf node. Once a leaf node is found, the new node is added as a child of the leaf node. The below steps are followed while we try to insert a node into a binary search tree:

* Check the value to be inserted (say X) with the value of the current node (say val) we are in:

    - If X is less than val move to the left subtree.

    - Otherwise, move to the right subtree.

* Once the leaf node is reached, insert X to its right or left based on the relation between X and the leaf node's value.

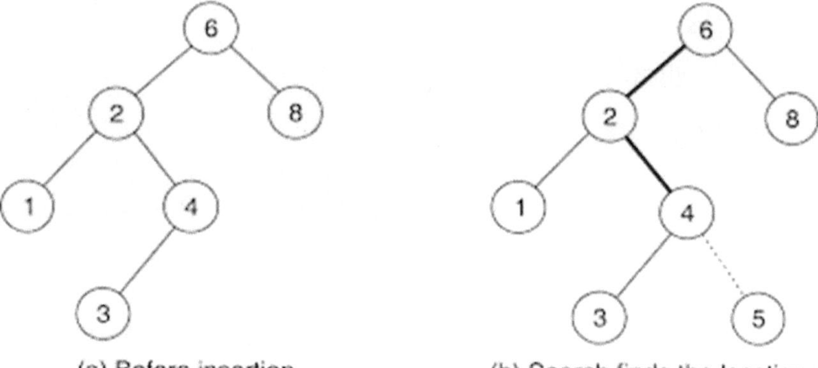

Figure 4.12: Inserting 5 in a Binary Search Tree

Algorithm Insert_BST

Input: ITEM is the data component of a node that has to be inserted
Output: If there is no node having ITEM, it is inserted into the tree else a message
Data structure: Linked structure of binary tree. Pointer to the root node is ROOT.

```
1.  Start
2.  Create a node NEW and insert ITEM in it.
3.  If( ROOT==null)
4.           Set ROOT=NEW
5.  Else
6.           Set ptr= ROOT
7.  while( ptr   !=   null )
8.           Set parent= ptr
9.           if( ITEM< ptr->data)
10.                  ptr=ptr->LCHILD
11.              if( ptr==null )
12.                      parent->LCHILD=temp
13.          else
14.                      ptr= ptr->RCHILD
15.                     if (ptr==null)
16.                     parent->RCHILD= temp
```

Deletion in a BST

There are the following possible cases when we delete a node:

1. The node to be deleted has **no children**. In this case, all we need to do is delete the node.

2. The node to be deleted has only **one child (left or right subtree)**. We delete the node and attach the subtree to the deleted node's parent.

3. The node to be deleted has **two children**. It is possible to delete a node from the middle of a tree, but the result tends to create very unbalanced trees.

Case 1: The node to be deleted has no children

The Node to be Deleted in Binary Search Tree is a Leaf Node. This is the simplest scenario. Simply replace the leaf node with NULL/None and release the space that has been allotted.
If we want to delete 27 we will replace this with None/Null.

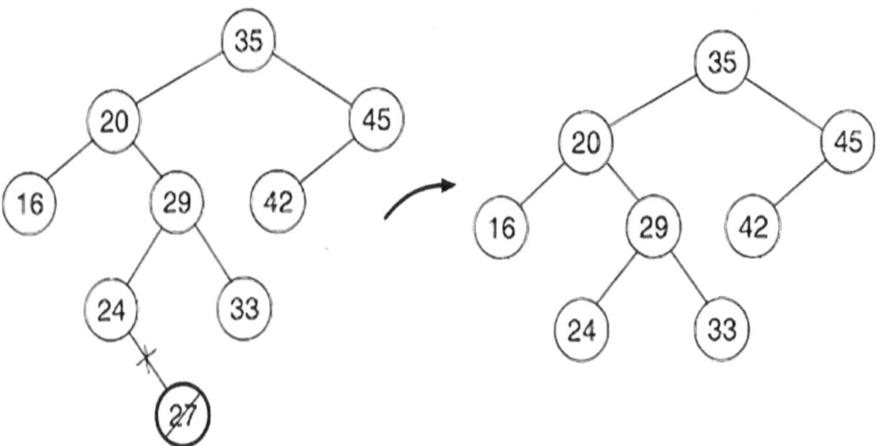

Figure 4.13: Deletion of Node 27

Case 2: The node to be deleted has exactly one child
Replace the node in this instance with its child and then remove the child node because it now has the value that needs to be destroyed. Simply replace it with NULL to release the space that was allotted.

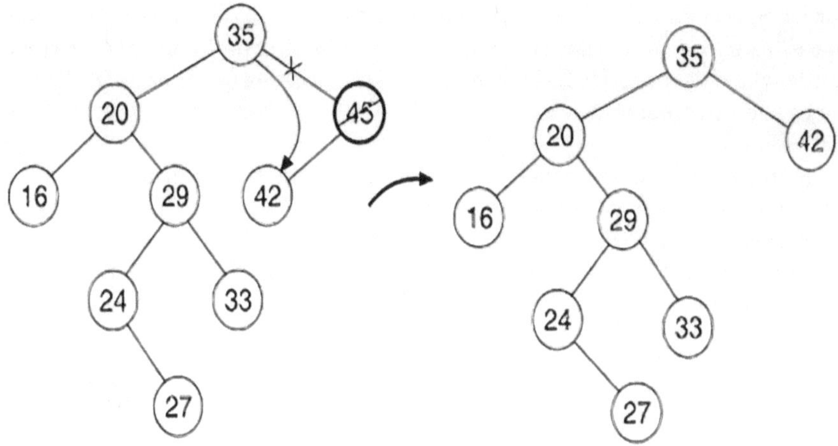

Figure 4.14: Deletion of Node 45

In the above BST if we want to delete 45 then we replace it with 42, by copying 42 to the node 45 and remove 42 as leaf node.

Case 3: The node to be deleted has two children
Compared to the previous two situations, it is a little more complicated. However, until the node value (to be deleted) is placed on the leaf of the tree, the node that is to be removed is replaced by its in-order successor or predecessor recursively.

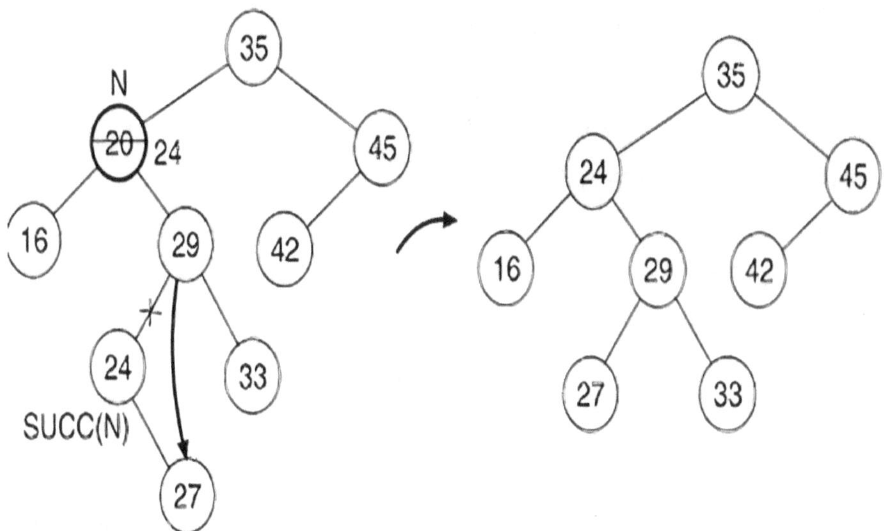

Figure 4.15: Deletion of Node 20

Inorder Successor: The following node in the Binary Tree's inorder traversal is referred to as a node's inorder successor. For the final node in an inorder traversal, inorder Successor is NULL. Inorder successor is the left most node in the right subtree of the node being deleted.

In the above BST if we want to remove 20 then first we will find an inorder successor(To get a node which is just greater than the node to be deleted) so the inorder successor is 24 so we replace 20 (node to be deleted) with 24(inorder successor) and delete 24 . Inorder successor with no have left child. So it comes in either in Case 1 or Case 2 of deletion.

Algorithm Delete_BST

Input: ITEM is the data component of a node that has to be deleted
Output: node with ITEM as data is deleted from the binary Search Tree
Data structure: Linked structure of binary tree. Pointer to the root node is ROOT.

```
1. if ptr != null then do step 2 to 7
2. if item < (ptr -> data) then
      Delete(item,ptr->lchild)
3. else if item > (ptr -> data)
      Delete(item,ptr -> rchild)
4. else if ( ptr -> lchild = null) and ( ptr -> rchild = null)
    ptr = null // Deleting leaf node
5. else if (ptr -> lchild = null) then
              ptr = ptr -> rchild // Single child
6. else if (ptr -> rchild = null) then
              ptr = ptr -> lchild  // Single child
7. else           // Deleting if more children are present
      7 a. item = deletemin(ptr -> rchild)
      7 b. set ptr -> data = item
      7 c.  delete(item, ptr->rchild)
```

Algorithm deletemin(ptr)

```
1.if ptr -> lchild = null
2.      return ptr ->item
3. else
4.      return  deletemin(ptr -> lchild)
```

4.2   Graphs

A Graph is a non-linear data structure consisting of vertices and edges. The vertices are sometimes also referred to as nodes and the edges are lines or arcs that connect any two nodes in the graph.

Definition: A graph G is composed of 2 sets
(i) A set V , called the set of all vertices(or nodes) (ii) A set E, called the set of edges(or arcs). The graph is denoted by G(E, V).

Components of a Graph

<u>Vertices</u>: Vertices are the fundamental units of the graph. Sometimes, vertices are also known as vertex or nodes. Every node/vertex can be labeled or unlabeled.

<u>Edges</u>: Edges are drawn or used to connect two nodes of the graph. It can be ordered pair of nodes in a directed graph. Edges can connect any two nodes in any possible way. There are no rules. Sometimes, edges are also known as arcs. Every edge can be labeled/unlabeled.

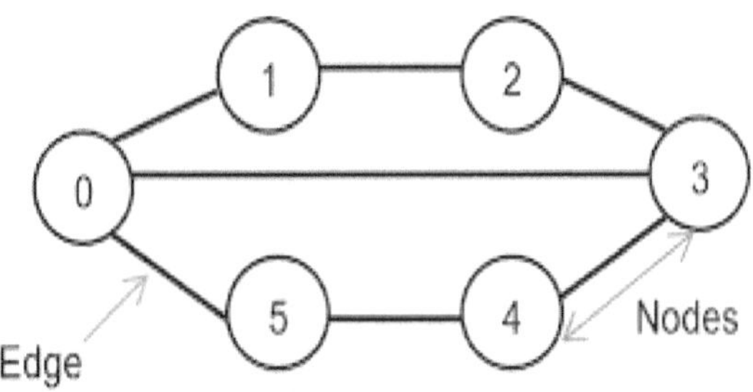

Figure 4.16: Graph

Graphs are used to solve many real-life problems. Graphs are used to represent networks. The networks may include paths in a city or telephone network or circuit network. Graphs are also used in social networks like LinkedIn, Facebook. For example, in Facebook, each person is represented with a vertex (or node). Each node is a structure and contains information like person id, name, gender, locale etc.

Tree is in fact, a special kind of graph structure. In tree structure, there is a hierarchical relationship between parent and children, that is, one parent and many children. On the other hand, in graph, relationship is less restricted. Here, relationship is from many parents to many children.

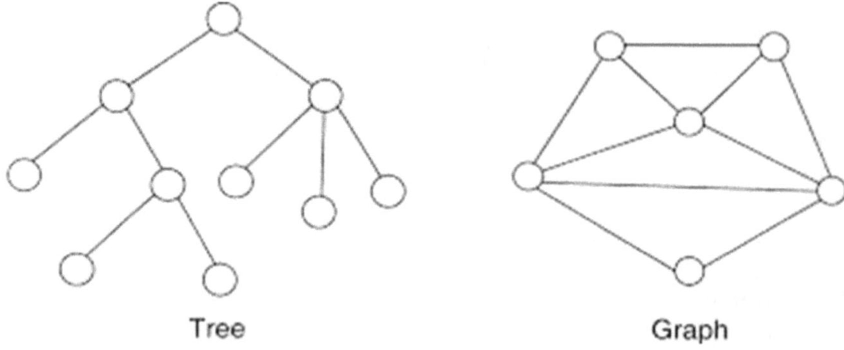

Tree   Graph

Figure 4.17: Tree and Graph: NonLinear Data Structure

4.2.1 Types of Graph

Undirected Graphs: A graph in which edges have no direction, i.e., the edges do not have arrows indicating the direction of traversal. Example: A social network graph where friendships are not directional.

Directed Graphs: A graph in which edges have a direction, i.e., the edges have arrows indicating the direction of traversal. Example: A web page graph where links between pages are directional.

Weighted Graphs: A graph in which edges have weights or costs associated with them. Example: A road network graph where the weights can represent the distance between two cities.
Unweighted Graphs: A graph in which edges have no weights or costs associated with them. Example: A social network graph where the edges represent friendships.

Cycles: A graph with at least one cycle. Example: A bike-sharing graph where the cycles represent the routes that the bikes take.

Sparse Graphs: A graph with relatively few edges compared to the number of vertices. Example: A chemical reaction graph where each vertex represents a chemical compound and each edge represents a reaction between two compounds.
Dense Graphs: A graph with many edges compared to the number of vertices. Example: A social network graph where each vertex represents a person and each edge represents a friendship.

Simple Graph: A simple graph is a graph that does not contain more than one edge between the pair of vertices. A simple railway track connecting different cities is an example of a simple graph.
Multi Graph: Any graph which contains some parallel edges but doesn't contain

112

any self-loop is called a multigraph. For example, a Road Map.

Parallel Edges: If two vertices are connected with more than one edge then such edges are called parallel edges that are many routes but one destination.

Loop: An edge of a graph that starts from a vertex and ends at the same vertex is called a loop or a self-loop.

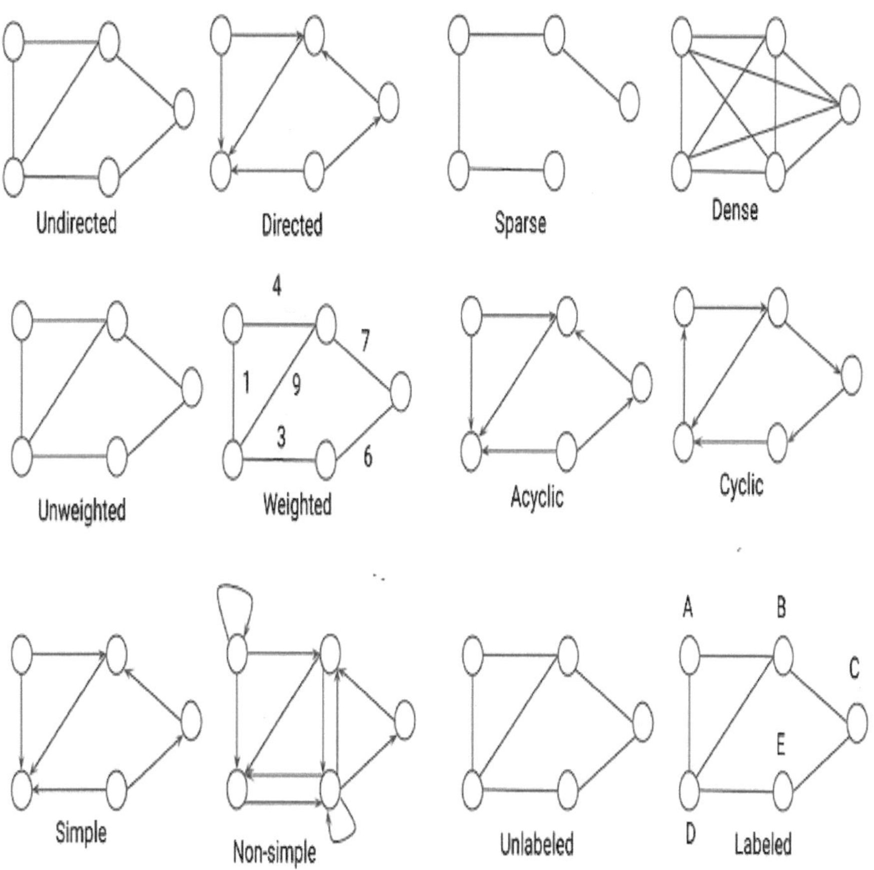

Figure 4.18: Types of Graph

Complete Graph: A simple graph with n vertices is called a complete graph if the degree of each vertex is n-1, that is, one vertex is attached with n-1 edges or the rest of the vertices in the graph. A complete graph is also called Full Graph.

Labeled Graph: If the vertices and edges of a graph are labeled with name, date, or weight then it is called a labeled graph. It is also called Weighted Graph.

Digraph Graph:
A graph G = (V, E) with a mapping f such that every edge maps onto some ordered pair of vertices (Vi, Vj) are called a Digraph. It is also called Directed Graph. The ordered pair (Vi, Vj) means an edge between Vi and Vj with an arrow directed from Vi to Vj. Here in the figure: e1 = (V1, V2) e2 = (V2, V3) e4 = (V2, V4)

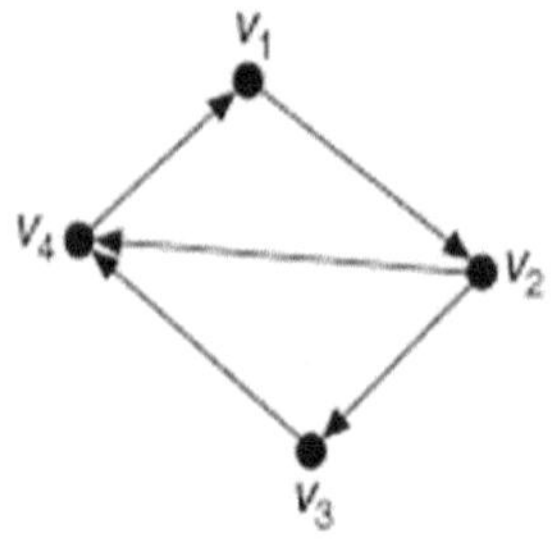

Figure 4.19: Directed Graph

Degree of vertex :- The number of edges connected with the vertex V_i and is denoted by degree(V_i)=3,$\forall$ $v_i \in$ for an undirected graph (Figure 4.21 (i)).

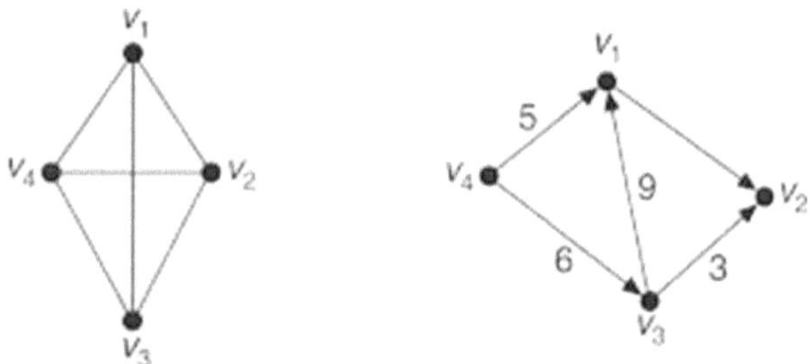

Figure 4.20: (i)Undirected Graph (ii) Directed Graph

But for a digraph / directed Graph, there are two degrees: indegree and out-degree.
Indegree of v_i denoted as indegree(v_i) = number of edges incident into v_i. similarly, outdegree(v_i) = number of edges emanating from v_i.
For example, let us consider the diagraph (Figure 4.21 (ii)), Here:

$$\begin{aligned}
\text{indegree}(v_1)&=2 & \text{outdegree}(v_1)&=1 \\
\text{indegree}(v_2)&=2 & \text{outdegree}(v_2)&=0 \\
\text{indegree}(v_3)&=1 & \text{outdegree}(v_3)&=2 \\
\text{indegree}(v_4)&=0 & \text{outdegree}(v_4)&=2
\end{aligned}$$

Advantages of graphs:

1. Graphs can be used to model and analyze complex systems and relationships.

2. They are useful for visualizing and understanding data.

3. Graph algorithms are widely used in computer science and other fields, such as social network analysis, logistics, and transportation.

4. Graphs can be used to represent a wide range of data types, including social networks, road networks, and the internet.

Disadvantages of graphs:

1. Large graphs can be difficult to visualize and analyze.

2. Graph algorithms can be computationally expensive, especially for large graphs.

3. The interpretation of graph results can be subjective and may require domain-specific knowledge.

4. Graphs can be susceptible to noise and outliers, which can impact the accuracy of analysis results.

4.2.2 Representation of Graphs

A graph can be represented as

1. Set representation

2. Linked representation

3. Adjacency matrix representation

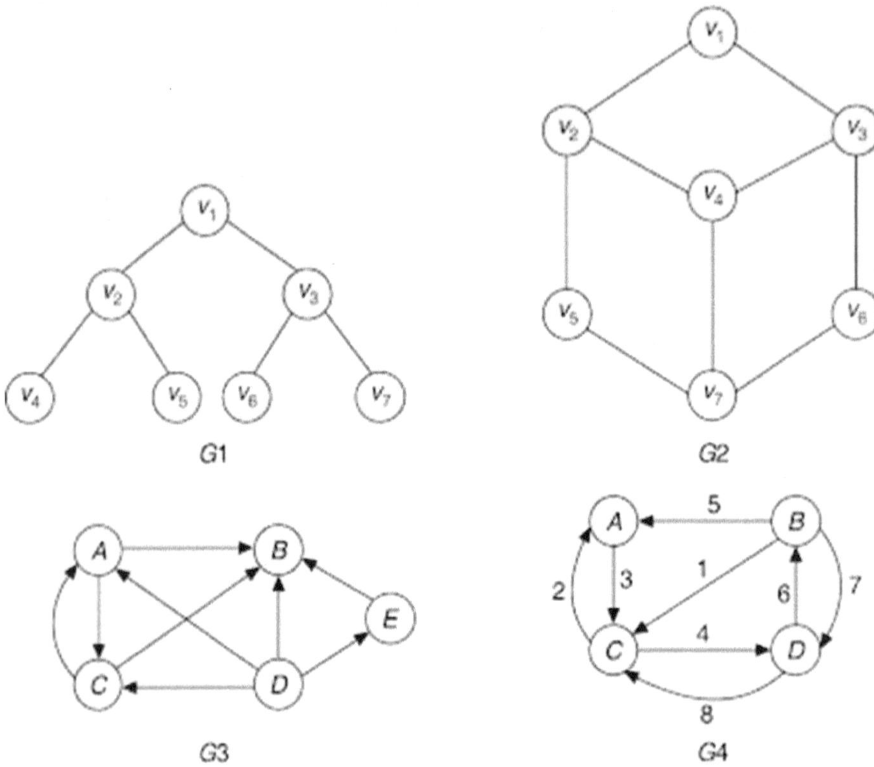

Figure 4.21: (i) G1: Tree Graph   (ii) G2: Undirected Graph
(iii) G3: Directed Graph   (iv) G4: W Weighted Graph

Set representation

This is one of the straightforward methods of representing a graph. With this method, two sets are maintained: (i) V, the set of vertices, (ii) E, the set of edges, which is the subset of $V \times V$. But if the graph is weighted, the set E is the ordered collection of three tuples, that is, $E = W \times V \times V$, where W is the set of weights.

Let us see, how all the graphs given in Figure   can be represented with this technique.

Graph G1

$\quad V(G1) = \{v_1, v_2, v_3, v_4, v_5, v_6, v_7\}$

$\quad E(G1) = \{(v_1, v_2), (v_1, v_3), (v_2, v_4), (v_2, v_5), (v_3, v_6), (v_3, v_7)\}$

Graph G2

$\quad V(G2) = \{v_1, v_2, v_3, v_4, v_5, v_6, v_7\}$

$\quad E(G2) = \{(v_1, v_2), (v_1, v_3), (v_2, v_4), (v_2, v_5), (v_3, v_4), (v_3, v_6), (v_4, v_7), (v_5, v_7), (v_6, v_7)\}$

Graph G3

$\quad V(G3) = \{A, B, C, D, E\}$

$\quad E(G3) = \{(A, B), (A, C), (C, B), (C, A), (D, A), (D, B), (D, C), (D, E), (E, B)\}$

Graph G4

$\quad V(G4) = \{A, B, C, D\}$

$\quad E(G4) = \{(3, A, C), (5, B, A), (1, B, C), (7, B, D), (2, C, A), (4, C, D), (6, D, B), (8, D, C)\}$

Note that, if the graph is a multigraph and undirected, this method does not allow to store parallel edges, as in a set, two identical elements cannot exist.

Linked representation

Linked representation is another space saving way of graph representation. In this representation, two types of nodes structures are assumed as show in Figure 4.23

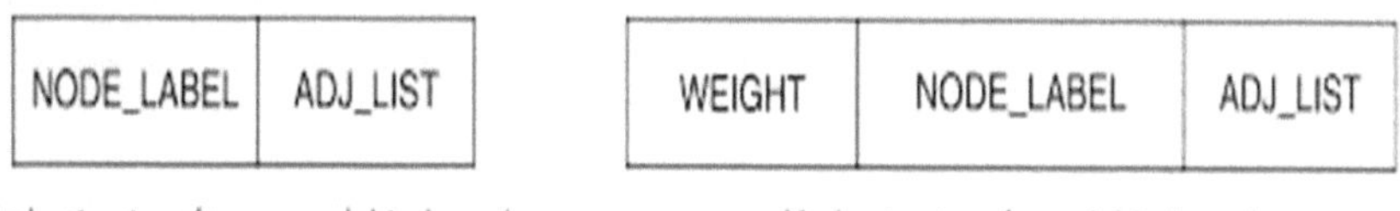

Figure 4.22: Node structure in Linked Representation for non weighted and weighted Graph

A linked representation is maintained as an adjacency list. In this representation, we keep a list of neighbors for each vertex in the graph. It means that each vertex in the graph has a list of its neighbors. Each array element points to a singly linked list of v's neighbors, and the array is indexed by the vertex number.

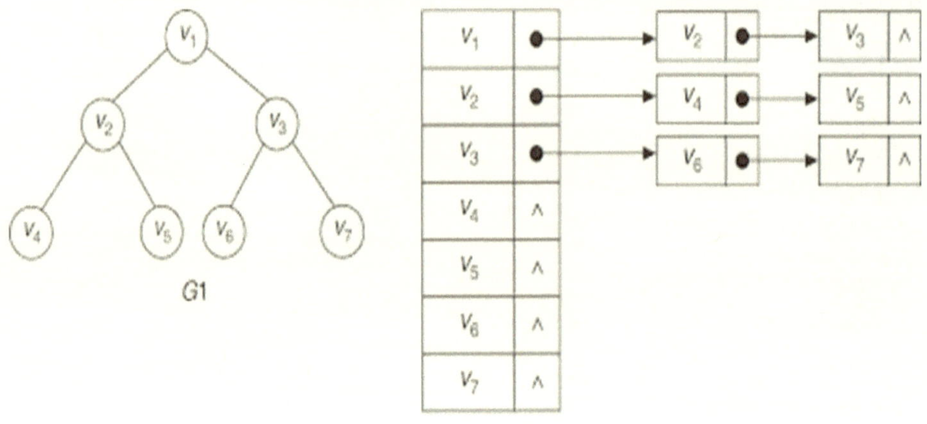

Figure 4.23: Linked Representation for Graph G1

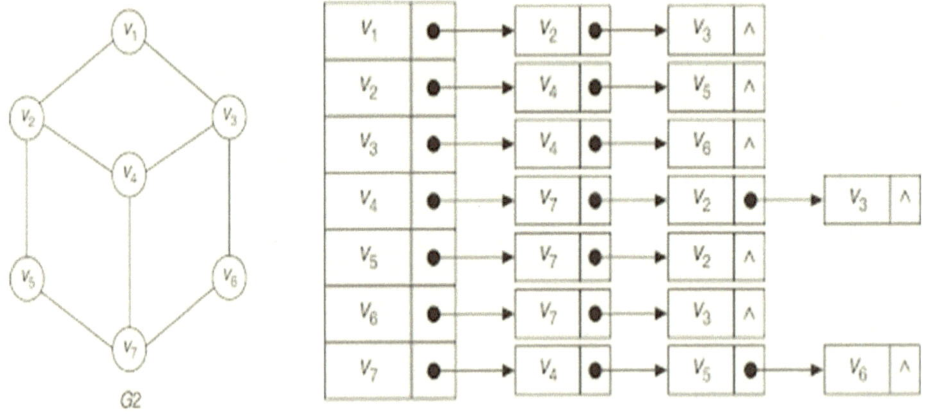

Figure 4.24: Linked Representation for Graph G2

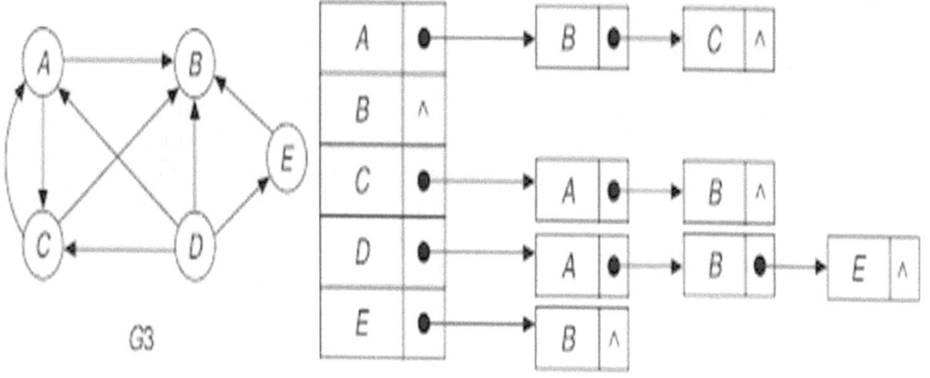

Figure 4.25: Linked Representation for Graph G3

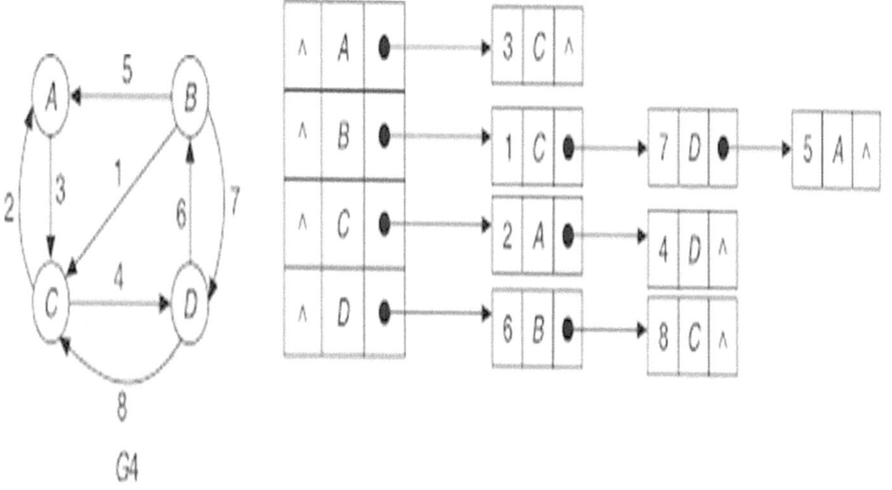

Figure 4.26: Linked Representation for Graph G4

Adjacency matrix representation

An adjacency matrix is a type of sequential representation.

It is used to indicate which nodes are adjacent to one another. I.e., do any edges connect nodes in a graph. In this representation, an NxN matrix, A[N][N] must be created. If an edge connects vertex i and vertex j, the corresponding element of A is A[i,j] = 1, otherwise, it is A[i,j] = 0. If there is a weighted graph, we can store the edge weight instead of 1s and 0s.

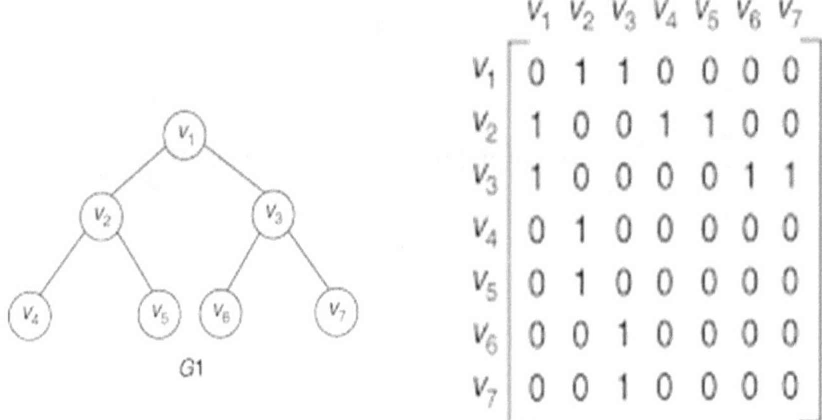

Figure 4.27: Adjacency Matrix Representation for Graph G1

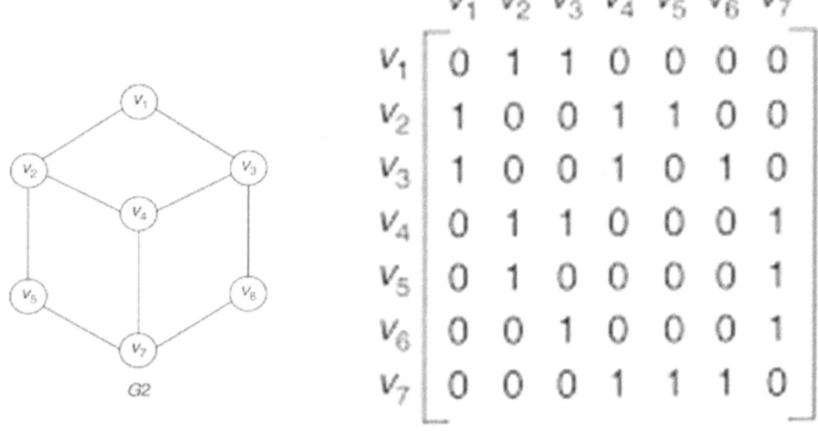

Figure 4.28: Adjacency Matrix Representation for Graph G2

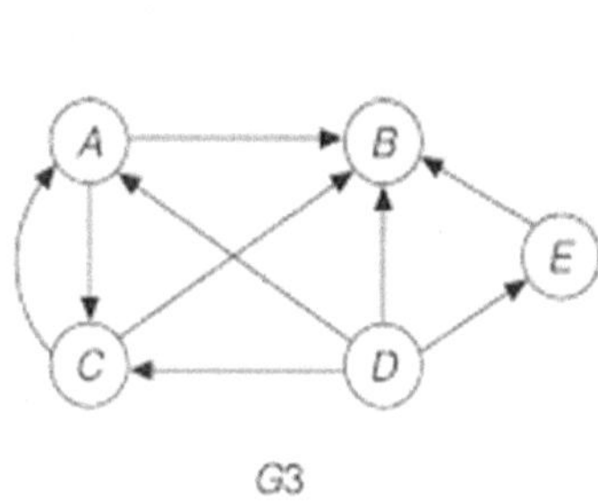

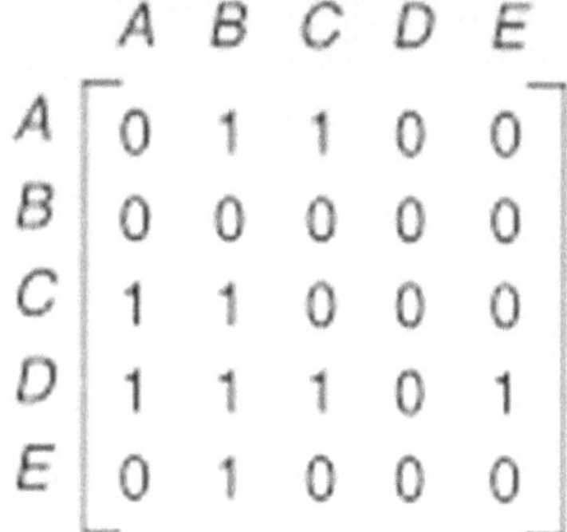

Figure 4.29: Adjacency Matrix Representation for Graph G3

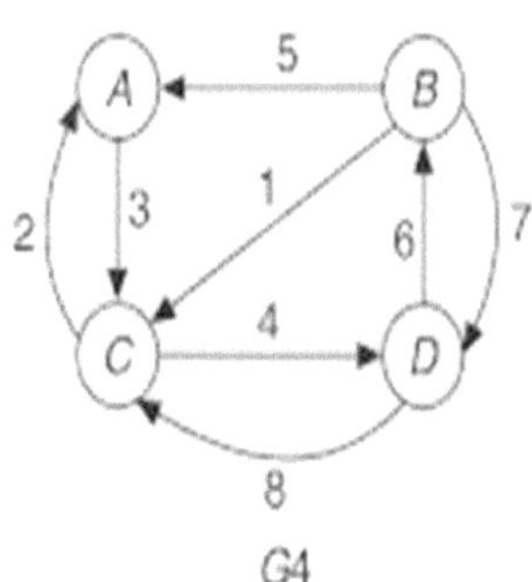

Figure 4.30: Adjacency Matrix Representation for Graph G4

4.2.3 Graph Traversal

There are 2 types of traversals:

1. Breadth First search

2. Depth First Search

BREADTH-FIRST SEARCH

The Breadth First Search (BFS) algorithm is used to search a graph data structure for a node that meets a set of criteria. It starts at the root of the graph and visits all nodes at the current depth level before moving on to the nodes at the next depth level. To avoid processing a node more than once, we divide the vertices into Visited and Not visited vertices. A Boolean visited array is used to mark the visited vertices. For simplicity, it is assumed that all vertices are reachable from the starting vertex.

Starting from the root, all the nodes at a particular level are visited first and then the nodes of the next level are traversed till all the nodes are visited.

To do this a queue is used. All the adjacent unvisited nodes of the current level are pushed into the queue and the nodes of the current level are marked visited and popped from the queue.

<u>Illustration:</u>

Let us understand the working of the algorithm with the help of the following example.

Step1: Initially queue and visited arrays are empty.

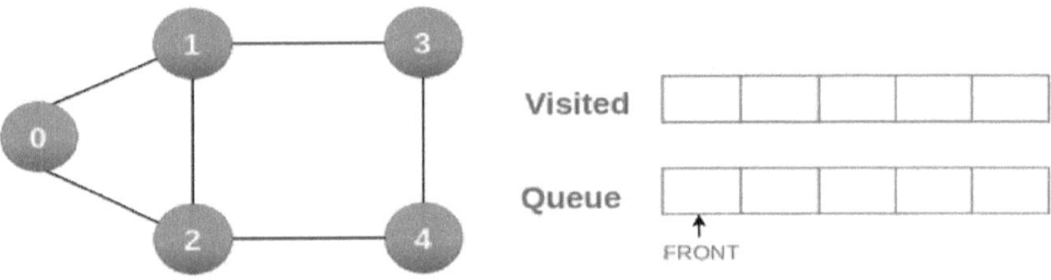

Step2: Push node 0 into queue and mark it visited.

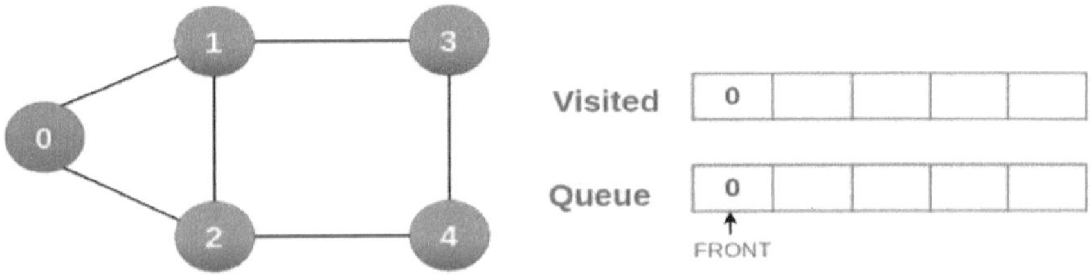

Step 3: Remove node 0 from the front of queue and visit the unvisited neighbours and push them into queue.

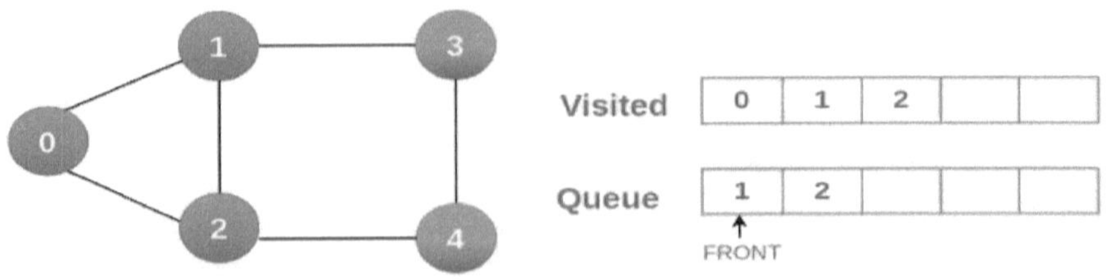

Step 4: Remove node 1 from the front of queue and visit the unvisited neighbours and push them into queue.

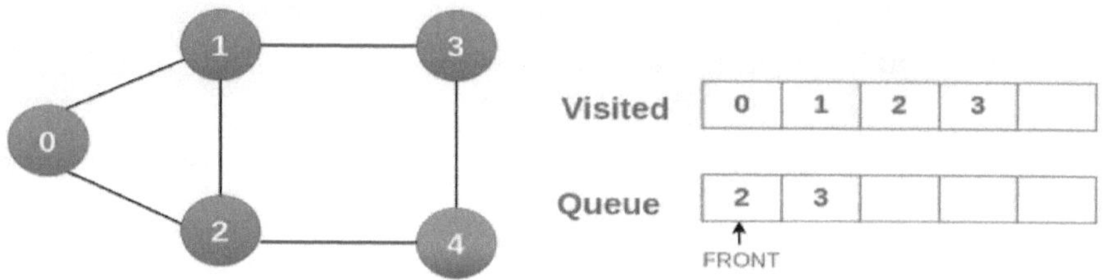

Step 5: Remove node 2 from the front of queue and visit the unvisited neighbours and push them into queue.

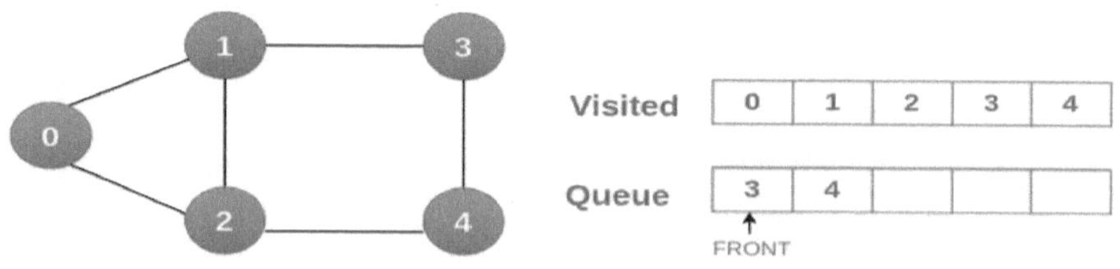

Step 6: Remove node 3 from the front of queue and visit the unvisited neighbours and push them into queue. As we can see that every neighbours of node 3 is visited, so move to the next node that are in the front of the queue.

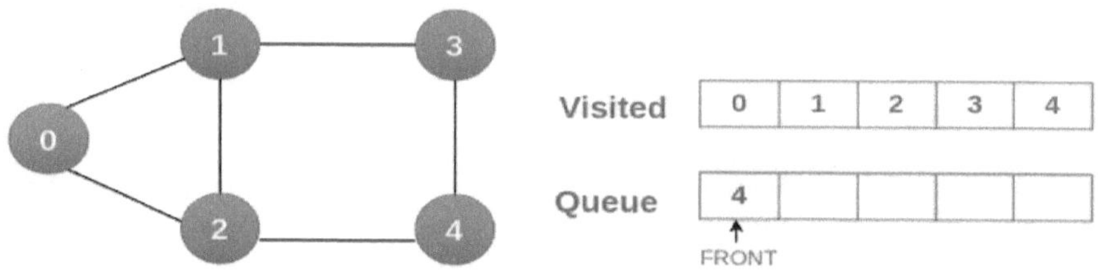

Steps 7: Remove node 4 from the front of queue and visit the unvisited neighbours and push them into queue. As we can see that every neighbours of node 4 are visited, and Queue becomes empty. So, terminate this process of iteration.

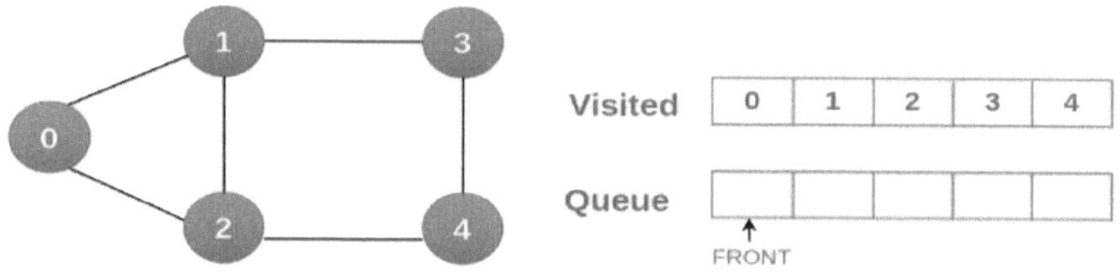

Steps
1. Initialize all the nodes as unvisited
2. Insert the first node/ starting node Vi to queue
3. Repeat 4 and 5 until queue is empty
4. Delete the node from Queue and mark it as visited
5. Insert the unvisited adjacent nodes of Vi to queue
6. Repeat until all the nodes are visited
7. Stop

DEPTH-FIRST SEARCH

Here the data structure used is STACK

Step1: Initially stack and visited arrays are empty.

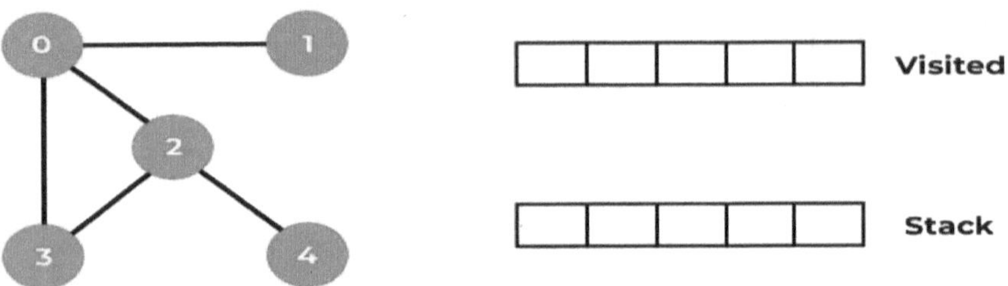

Step 2: Visit 0 and put its adjacent nodes which are not visited yet into the stack.

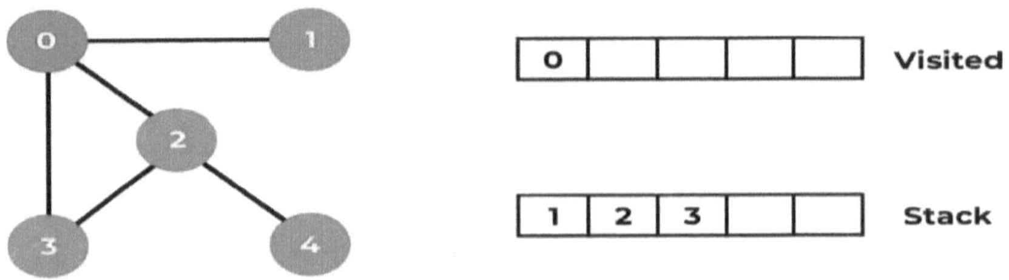

Step 3: Now, Node 1 at the top of the stack, so visit node 1 and pop it from the stack and put all of its adjacent nodes which are not visited in the stack.

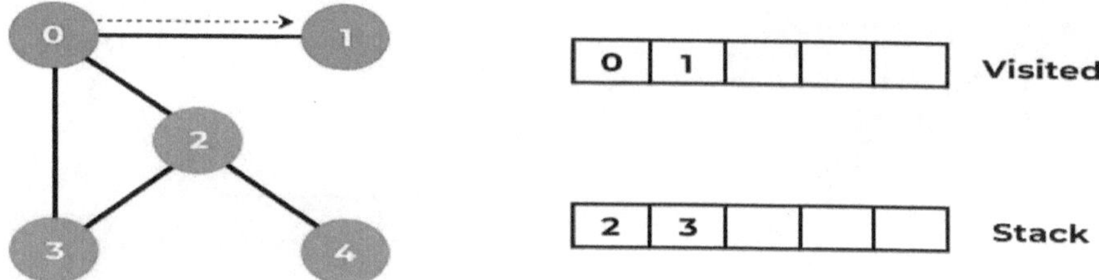

Step 4: Now, Node 2 at the top of the stack, so visit node 2 and pop it from the stack and put all of its adjacent nodes which are not visited (i.e, 3, 4) in the stack.

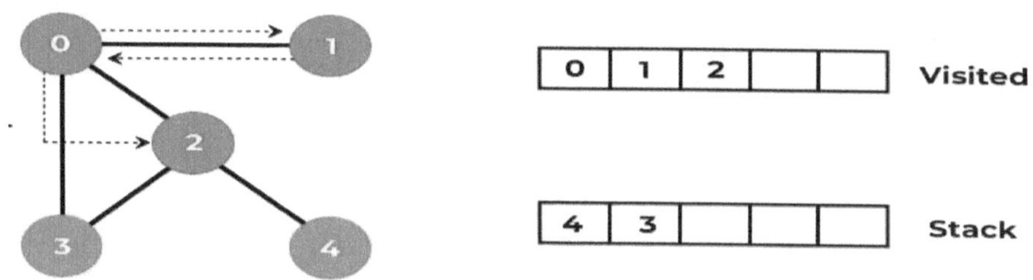

Step 5: Now, Node 4 at the top of the stack, so visit node 4 and pop it from the stack and put all of its adjacent nodes which are not visited in the stack.

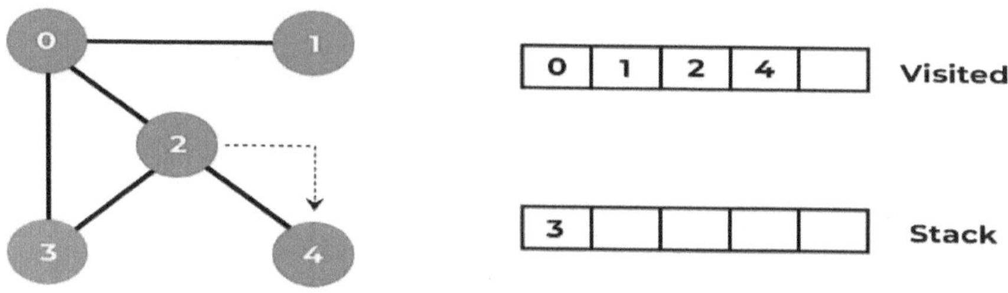

Step 6: Now, Node 3 at the top of the stack, so visit node 3 and pop it from the stack and put all of its adjacent nodes which are not visited in the stack.

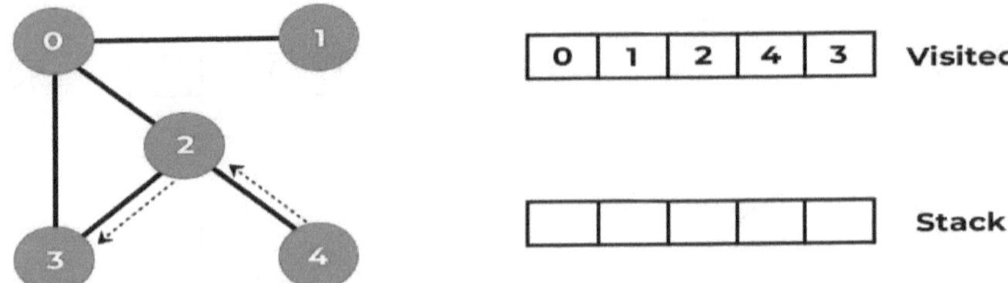

Algorithm

```
Steps
1. Initialize all the nodes as visited
2. PUSH the first node/ starting node Vi to stack
3. Repeat 4 and 5 until stack is empty
4. POP the top node of stack Vi and mark it as visited
5. PUSH the unvisited adjacent nodes of Vi to stack
6. Repeat until all the nodes are visited
7. Stop
```

4.2.4   Application of Graph

Travelling Sales Man Problem

Travelling salesman problem takes a graph G V, E as an input and declare another graph as the output (say G') which will record the path the salesman is going to take from one node to another.

- The algorithm begins by sorting all the edges in the input graph G from the least distance to the largest distance.

- The first edge selected is the edge with least distance, and one of the two vertices (say A and B) being the origin node (say A). Then among the adjacent edges of the node other than the origin node (B), find the least cost edge and add it onto the output graph.

- Continue the process with further nodes making sure there are no cycles in the output graph and the path reaches back to the origin node A.

However, if the origin is mentioned in the given problem, then the solution must always start from that node only.

Consider the following graph with six cities and the distances between them :

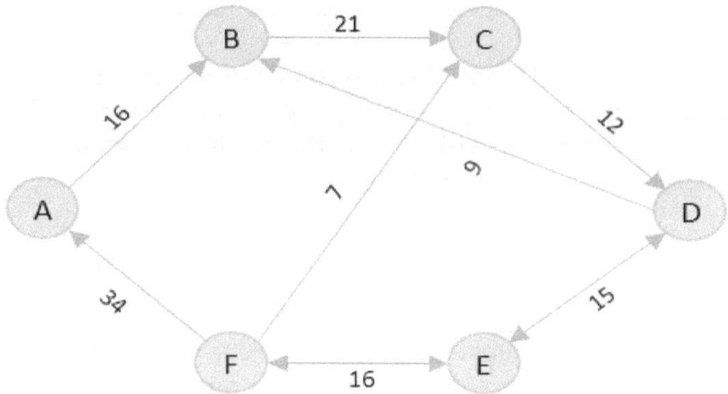

From the given graph, since the origin is already mentioned, the solution must always start from that node. Among the edges leading from A, A − > B has the shortest distance. Then, B − > C has the shortest and only edge between B − > C , therefore it is included in the output graph. There's only one edge between C − > D, therefore it is added to the output graph. There's two outward edges from D. Even though, D − > B has lower distance than D − > E, B is already visited once and it would form a cycle if added to the output graph. Therefore, D − > E is added into the output graph. There's only one edge from E, that is E − > F. Therefore, it is added into the output graph. Again, even though F − > C has lower distance than F − > A, F − > A is added into the output graph in order to avoid the cycle that would form and C is already visited once.

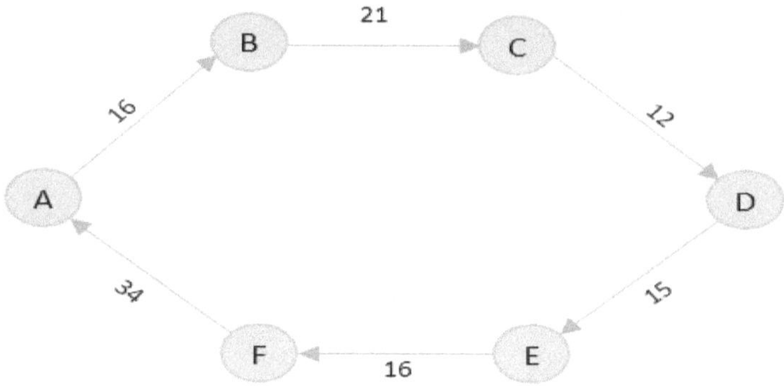

The shortest path that originates and ends at A is

A − > B − > C − > D − > E − > F − > A

The cost of the path is: 16 + 21 + 12 + 15 + 16 + 34 = 114.

Topological Sorting

Topological sort is a technique used in graph theory to order the vertices of a directed acyclic graph (DAG). It ensures that for every directed edge from vertex A to vertex B, vertex A comes before vertex B in the ordering. This is useful in scheduling problems, where tasks depend on the completion of other tasks.

The algorithm begins by selecting a vertex with no incoming edges, adding it to the ordering, and removing all outgoing edges from the vertex. This process is repeated until all vertices are visited, and the resulting ordering is a topological sort of the DAG.The ordering of the nodes in the array is called a topological ordering.

Consider the following directed graph with 5 vertices.

Take a vertex with indegree=0. If vertex B is selected, remove the outgoing vertices from A from the graph. B− >E and $B− > C$ is removed.Now vertex E has indegree=0, so E is selected. Remove edges outgoing from E, E− >A and E− >C.

The process is repeated as shown in Figure below.

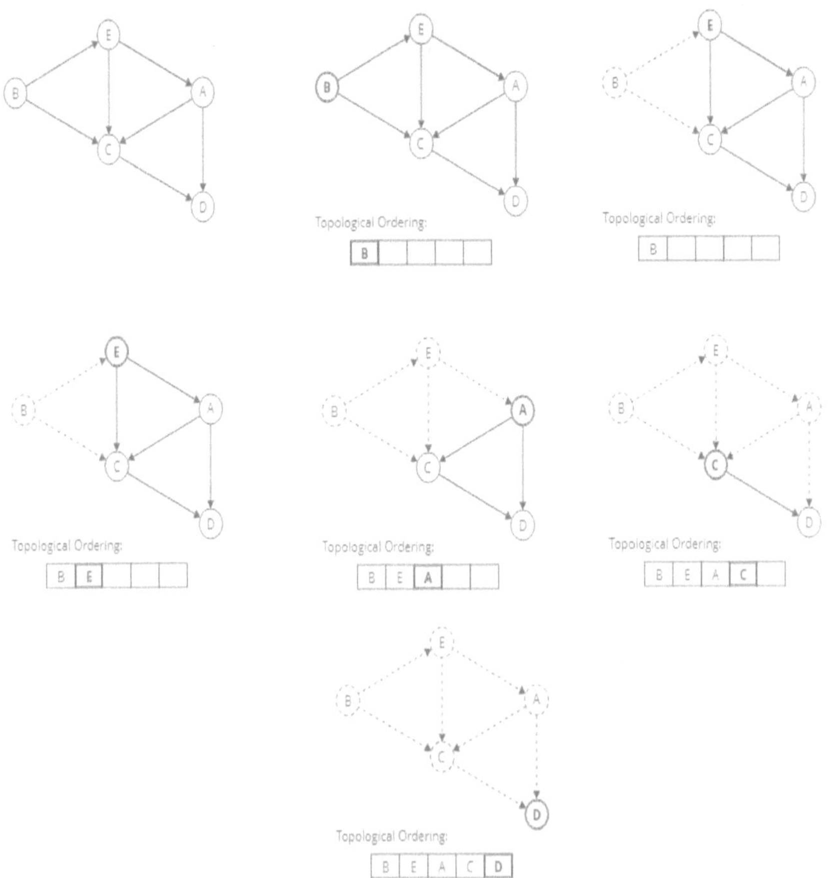

The topological ordering thus got is B− >E− >A− >C− >D

Minimum Spanning Tree

A minimum spanning tree (MST) is defined as a spanning tree that has the minimum weight among all the possible spanning trees.

A spanning tree is defined as a tree-like subgraph of a connected, undirected graph that includes all the vertices of the graph. It is a subset of the edges of the graph that forms a tree (acyclic) where every node of the graph is a part of the tree.

The minimum spanning tree has all the properties of a spanning tree with an added constraint of having the minimum possible weights among all possible spanning trees.

If you have graph G with vertices V and edges E, then that graph can be represented as G(V, E). For this graph G(V, E), if you construct a tree structure G'(V', E') such that the formed tree structure follows constraints mentioned below, then that structure can be called a Spanning Tree.

V' = V (number of Vertices in G' must be equal to the number of vertices in G)

E' = V - 1 (Edges of G' must be equal to the number of vertices in graph G minus 1)

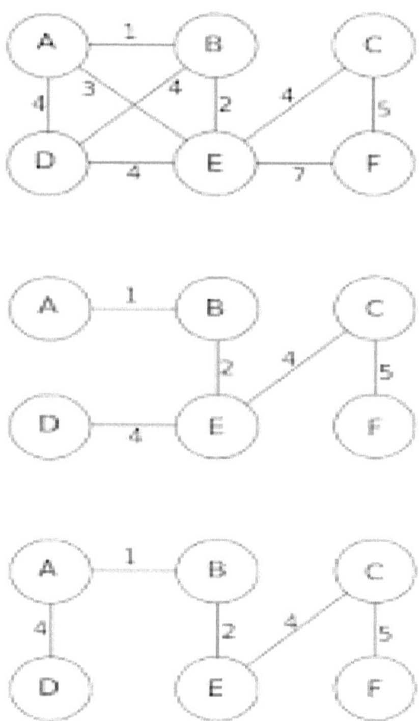

Figure 4.31: (i) Weighted undirected graph(ii) MST 1 (iii) MST 2

129

Kruskal's Algorithm

Kruskal's Algorithm is used for finding Minimum Spanning Trees. It starts by sorting all the edges of the graph in increasing order of their weights. Then, it takes each edge one by one and checks if adding the edge would create a cycle. If it doesn't, the edge is added to the MST. This process is repeated until all the vertices of the graph are included in the MST.

In the above example of Graph given in Figure 4.32 (i)

A− >B	1	Selected
B− >E	2	Selected
A− >E	3	Not selected as it forms a cycle
D− >E	4	Selected
D− >A	4	Not selected as it forms a cycle
D− >B	4	Not selected as it forms a cycle
E− >C	4	Selected
C− >F	5	Selected
E− >F	7	Not selected as it forms a cycle

This results in the MST1 showing in Figure 4.32 (ii). There can be more than one minimum Spanning Tree, depending on the selection of edges with same weight. Figure 4.32 (iii) shows another MST2

Module 5

5.1   Sorting

Sorting refers to arranging data in a particular format. A Sorting Algorithm is used to rearrange a given array or list of elements according to a comparison operator on the elements. The comparison operator is used to decide the new order of elements in the respective data structure. The list of elements can be arranged either in ascending or descending order.

Sorting Techniques can be classified into two Internal Sorting and External Sorting

* **Internal Sorting** : The internal sorting takes place entirely within the primary memory of a computer system. In this case the data is less in number and the sorting takes place in primary memory (RAM) itself. Insertion sorting is one of the examples of internal sorting.

* **External Sorting** : External sorting is a term for a class of sorting algorithms that can handle massive amounts of data The external sorting is taking place in the secondary memory. Firstly, the portion by potion data is transferred in the primary memory of a computer system then we sorting that data. Merge sort is one of the examples of external sorting.

5.1.1   Bubble Sort

Sorting is done by comparing adjacent elements of the list (array) and exchange (Swap) them if they are out of order.
In each pass, the current largest element is bubbled up to the last position.
After the first pass, the largest element is placed at the last position of the list.
Next pass bubbles up the second largest element, and so on until the list is sorted.
There will be n-1 passes.

Unsorted array	18	25	30	12	15
After first Pass	18	25	12	15	**<u>30</u>**
After Second Pass	18	12	15	**<u>25</u>**	30
After Third Pass	12	15	**<u>18</u>**	25	30
After Fourth Pass	12	**<u>15</u>**	18	25	30
Sorted Array	**12**	**15**	**18**	**25**	**30**

Figure 5.1: Different passes of bubble sort

Bubble Sort - Pseudocode

Let A[ ] be an array of n elements to be sorted in ascending order

```
bubblesort(int A[], int n)
{   for( i = 0;i < n-1; i++ )
      { for(j = 0 ; j < n-1-i ; j++)
          { if(a[ j ] > a[ j+1 ])
                        // Comparing adjacent Elements
                 {        t = a[ j ];      // Swapping
                          a[ j ] = a[ j+1 ];
                          a[ j+1 ] = t;
                 }
          }
      }
}
```

Complexity Analysis of Bubble Sort:

Time Complexity: $O(N^2)$ **Space Complexity:** $O(1)$

Advantages of Bubble Sort:

- Bubble sort is easy to understand and implement.

- It does not require any additional memory space.

- It is a stable sorting algorithm, meaning that elements with the same key value maintain their relative order in the sorted output.

Disadvantages of Bubble Sort:

- Bubble sort has a time complexity of $O(N^2)$ which makes it very slow for large data sets.

- Bubble sort is a comparison-based sorting algorithm, which means that it requires a comparison operator to determine the relative order of elements in the input data set. It can limit the efficiency of the algorithm in certain cases.

5.1.2   Selection Sort

Selection sort is done by scanning entire array to find its smallest element and exchange it with the first element.
In each pass we place the current smallest element in its exact position.
In first pass the smallest element of the list placed in its position (first position).
In second pass, the second smallest element is placed, and so on until the list is sorted.
Here also there will be n-1 passes.

Unsorted array	18	25	30	12	15
After first Pass	**12**	25	30	18	15
After Second Pass	12	**15**	30	18	25
After Third Pass	12	15	**18**	30	25
After Fourth Pass	12	15	18	**25**	30
Sorted Array	12	15	18	25	30

Figure 5.2: Different passes of selection sort

Let A[ ] be an array of n elements to be sorted in ascending order

```
selectionsort(int A[], int n)
{
  for ( i=0; i < n-1; i++ )              // counting no of passes
  {
     min = i;                   // assigning min as current first index
     for( j = i+1 ; j<n ; j++ )
      {
         if( a[min] > a[ j ] )
            min = j;
      }
     t = a[min];          //Swapping smallest element
     a[min] = a[i];       //and first element
     a[i] = t;
  }
}
```

Complexity Analysis of Selection Sort:

Time Complexity: $O(N^2)$

The time complexity of Selection Sort is $O(N^2)$ as there are two nested loops:
One loop to select an element of Array one by one = O(N)
Another loop to compare that element with every other Array element = O(N)

Therefore overall complexity = O(N) * O(N) = O(N*N) = $O(N^2)$

Space Complexity: O(1)

O(1) as the only extra memory used is for temporary variables while swapping two values in Array. The selection sort never makes more than O(N) swaps and can be useful when memory writing is costly.

Advantages of Selection Sort:

- Simple and easy to understand.

- Works well with small datasets.

Disadvantages of Selection Sort:

- Selection sort has a time complexity of $O(n^2)$ in the worst and average case.

- Does not work well on large datasets.

- Does not preserve the relative order of items with equal keys which means it is not stable.

5.1.3   Insertion Sort

Insertion sort is a simple sorting algorithm that works similar to the way you sort playing cards in your hands. The array is virtually split into a sorted and an unsorted part. Values from the unsorted part are picked and placed at the correct position in the sorted part.
Step 1 : The first element is assumed to be sorted.
Step 2 : Pick the next element.
Step 3 : Compare it with all elements in the sorted sub-list to the left of the element.
Step 4 : Shift elements that are greater than the picked element in the sorted sub-list.
Step 5 : Insert the value in the subsorted list.
Step 6 : Repeat until list is sorted.

Insertion Sort - Example

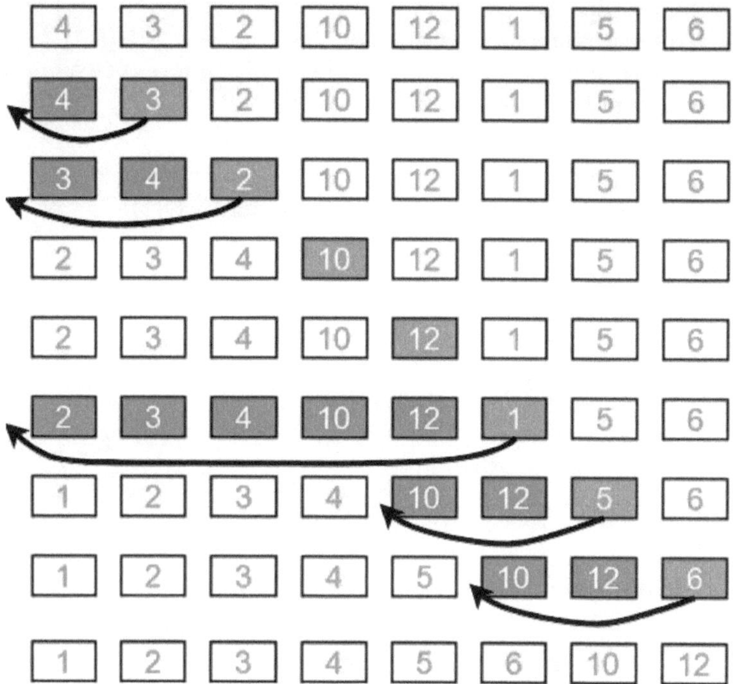

Figure 5.3: Different passes of insertion sort

Let A[ ] be an array of n elements to be sorted in ascending order

```
insertionSort(int A[], int n)
{
  for (i = 1; i < n; i++)
    {
        key = arr[i];
        j = i - 1;
        // Move elements of arr[0..i-1] that are greater than key,
        // to one position ahead of their current position.
        while (j >= 0 && arr[j] > key)
        {
            arr[j + 1] = arr[j];
            j = j - 1;
        }
        arr[j + 1] = key;
    }
}
```

Time Complexity: $O(N^2)$
The worst-case time complexity of the Insertion sort is $O(N^2)$.
The average case time complexity of the Insertion sort is $O(N^2)$.
The time complexity of the best case is O(N).

Space Complexity: O(1)
The auxiliary space complexity of Insertion Sort is O(1).

Characteristics of Insertion Sort

- This algorithm is one of the simplest algorithms with a simple implementation.

- Insertion sort is efficient for small data values.

- Insertion sort is adaptive in nature, i.e. it is appropriate for data sets that are already partially sorted.

- Insertion sort is a stable in-place sorting algorithm.

5.1.4   Merge Sort

Merge sort is an example of a divide-and-conquer algorithm. Divide-and-conquer algorithms solve complex problems by breaking them down into smaller sub-problems. Each sub-problem is then solved recursively, and the solutions are combined to get the final solution.

Merge sort is a recursive algorithm that continuously divides an array into two halves until it cannot be further divided i.e., the array has only one element left (an array with one element is always sorted), sorting each half, and then merging the sorted halves back together. This process is repeated until the subarrays are merged into one sorted array

Illustration:

Divide: Split your array of data in half, again and again, until each piece can't be divided further (you'll end up with arrays of just one element).

Conquer: Now, with each piece being sorted (since it's just one element), you start combining them.

Merge: As you combine these pieces, you sort them along the way. Think of merging two small stacks of cards where each stack is already in order.

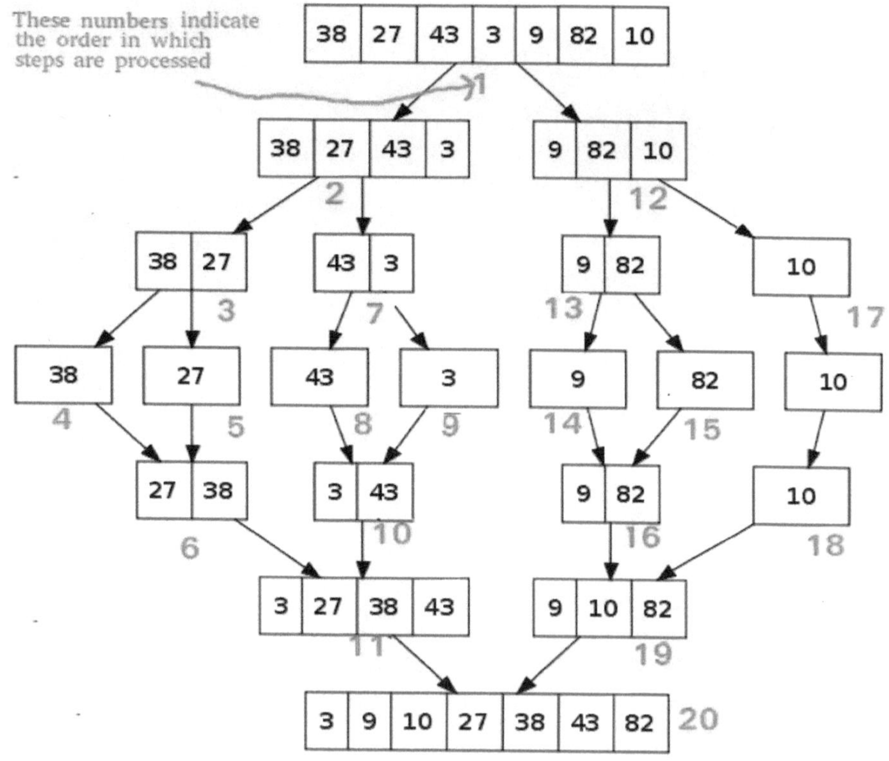

Figure 5.4: Different passes of Merge sort

Merge Sort - Pseudocode

Let A[ ] be an array of n elements to be sorted in ascending order.

```
Mergesort(A, low, high)
{
  if (low < high )
     { set mid = (low + high)/2
       Call   Mergesort(A, low, mid)
       Call   Mergesort(A, mid + 1, high)
       Call   Merge (A, low, mid, high)
     }
}
Merge(A, low, mid, high)
{
     I = low,
     J = mid + 1,
     index =0
```

Repeat **while** (I <= mid && J <= high)

    a. **if** (A[I] <= A[J])
        TEMP[index] = A[I]
        index= index+1
        I=I+1
    b. **else**
        TEMP[index] = A[J]
        index= index+1
        J=J+1
[end loop]

//copy remaining elements of left_sub array if any

Repeat **while** (I <= mid)

    TEMP[index] = A[I]
    index= index+1
    I=I+1
//copy remaining elements of right_sub array if any

Repeat **while** (J <= high)
    TEMP[index] = A[J]
    index= index+1
    J=J+1
//copy temp back to array A

Set K=0
Repeat **while** (K<index)
    a. set A[low+K] = TEMP[K];
    b. K=K+1
}

Complexity Analysis of Merge Sort:

Time Complexity: $O(Nlog(N))$
Merge Sort is a recursive algorithm and time complexity can be expressed as following recurrence relation.

$$T(n) = 2T(n/2) + \Theta(n)$$

The above recurrence can be solved either using the Recurrence Tree method or the Master method. It falls in case II of the Master Method and the solution of the recurrence is $\Theta(Nlog(N))$. The time complexity of Merge Sort is O(Nlog(N)) in all 3 cases (worst, average, and best) as merge sort always divides the array into two halves and takes linear time to merge two halves.

Space Complexity : O(N)

In merge sort all elements are copied into an auxiliary/temporary array. So N auxiliary space is required for merge sort.

Applications of Merge Sort

- Sorting large datasets: Merge sort is particularly well-suited for sorting large datasets due to its guaranteed worst-case time complexity of O(n log n).

- External sorting: Merge sort is commonly used in external sorting, where the data to be sorted is too large to fit into memory.

- Custom sorting: Merge sort can be adapted to handle different input distributions, such as partially sorted, nearly sorted, or completely unsorted data.

Advantages of Merge Sort:

- Stability: Merge sort is a stable sorting algorithm, which means it maintains the relative order of equal elements in the input array.

- Guaranteed worst-case performance: Merge sort has a worst-case time complexity of O(N logN), which means it performs well even on large datasets.

- Parallelizable: Merge sort is a naturally parallelizable algorithm, which means it can be easily parallelized to take advantage of multiple processors or threads.

Disadvantages of Merge Sort:

- Space complexity: Merge sort requires additional memory to store the merged sub-arrays during the sorting process.

- Not in-place: Merge sort is not an in-place sorting algorithm, which means it requires additional memory to store the sorted data. This can be a disadvantage in applications where memory usage is a concern.

- Not always optimal for small datasets: For small datasets, Merge sort has a higher time complexity than some other sorting algorithms, such as insertion sort. This can result in slower performance for very small datasets.

5.1.5   Quick Sort

Quicksort is a sorting algorithm based on the Divide and Conquer algorithm that picks an element as a pivot and partitions the given array around the picked pivot by placing the pivot in its correct position in the array.

The key process in quickSort is a partition(). The target of partitions is to place the pivot at its correct position in the array such that all smaller elements are placed to the left of the pivot, and all greater elements are to the right of the pivot. Either first or last can b taken as pivot, here we consider first element of each subarray(partition) as pivot. Partition is done recursively on each side of the pivot after the pivot is placed in its correct position and this finally sorts the array.

In Quick sort algorithm, partitioning of the list is performed using following steps.

Step 1 - Consider the first element of the list as pivot (i.e., Element at first position in the list).

Step 2 - Define two variables i and j. Set i and j to first and last elements of the list respectively.

Step 3 - Increment i until list[i] > pivot then stop.

Step 4 - Decrement j until list[j] < pivot then stop.

Step 5 - If i < j then exchange list[i] and list[j].

Step 6 - Repeat steps 3,4 and 5 until i > j.

Step 7 - Exchange the pivot element with list[j] element.

Figure 1.5 shows that 54 will serve as our first pivot value. Since we have looked at this example a few times already, we know that 54 will eventually end up in the position currently holding 31. The partition process will happen next. It will find the split point and at the same time move other items to the appropriate side of the list, either less than or greater than the pivot value.

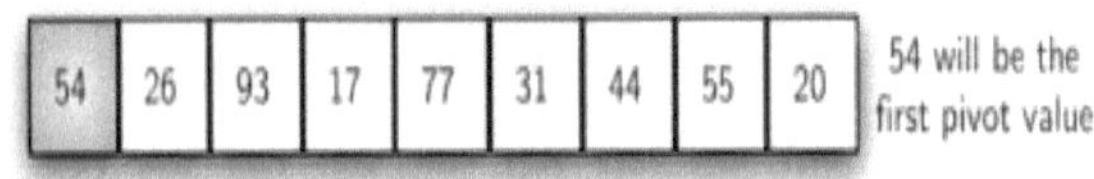

Figure 5.5: The First Pivot Value for a Quick Sort

Partitioning begins by locating two position markers—let's call them leftmark and rightmark—at the beginning and end of the remaining items in the list (positions 1 and 8 in Figure 13). The goal of the partition process is to move items that are on the wrong side with respect to the pivot value while also converging on the split point. Figure 13 shows this process as we locate the position of 54.

We begin by incrementing leftmark until we locate a value that is greater than the pivot value. We then decrement rightmark until we find a value that is less than the pivot value. At this point we have discovered two items that are out of place with respect to the eventual split point. For our example, this occurs at 93 and 20. Now we can exchange these two items and then repeat the process again.

At the point where rightmark becomes less than leftmark, we stop. The position of rightmark is now the split point. The pivot value can be exchanged with the contents of the split point and the pivot value is now in place (Figure 14). In addition, all the items to the left of the split point are less than the pivot value,

and all the items to the right of the split point are greater than the pivot value.
The list can now be divided at the split point and the quick sort can be invoked
recursively on the two halves.

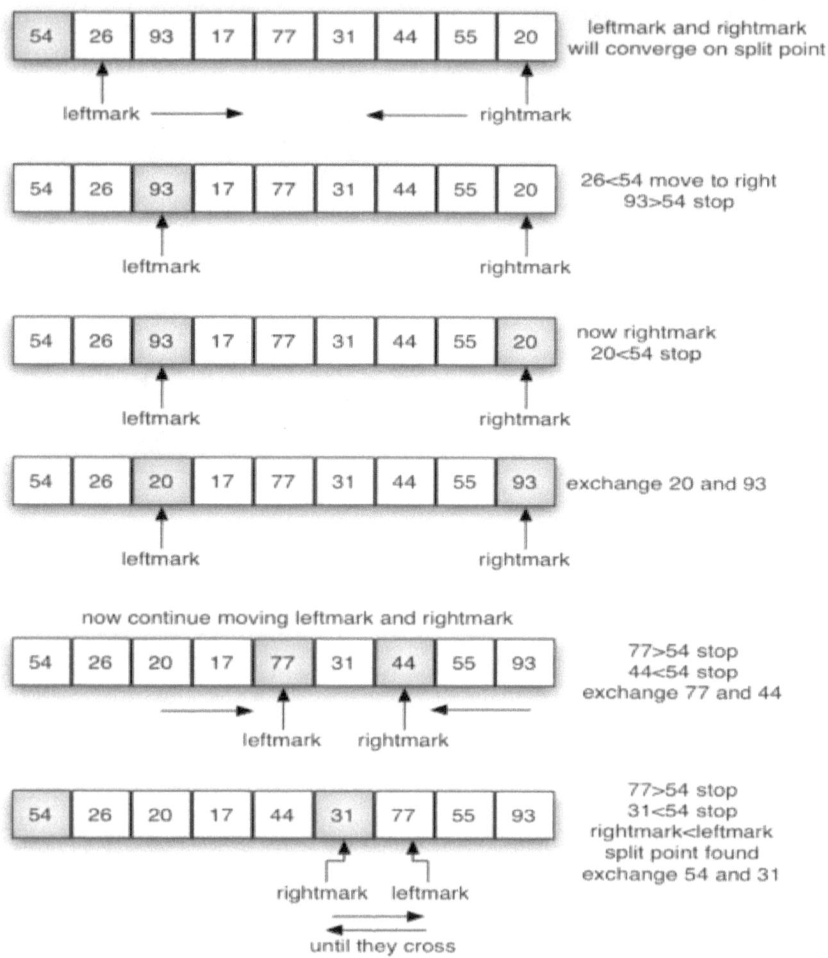

Figure 5.6: Finding the Split Point for 54

We begin by incrementing leftmark until we locate a value that is greater than
the pivot value. We then decrement rightmark until we find a value that is less
than the pivot value. At this point we have discovered two items that are out of
place with respect to the eventual split point. For our example, this occurs at 93
and 20. Now we can exchange these two items and then repeat the process again.

At the point where rightmark becomes less than leftmark, we stop. The position of rightmark is now the split point. The pivot value can be exchanged with

the contents of the split point and the pivot value is now in place (Figure 14). In addition, all the items to the left of the split point are less than the pivot value, and all the items to the right of the split point are greater than the pivot value. The list can now be divided at the split point and the quick sort can be invoked recursively on the two halves.

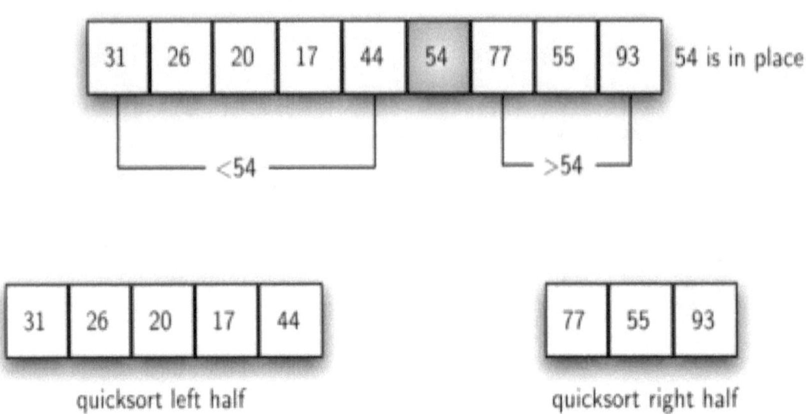

Figure 5.7: Completing the Partition Process to Find the Split Point for 54

Quick Sort - Pseudocode

Let A[ ] be an array of n elements to be sorted in ascending order.

```
QuickSort(A,beg,end)
{
    If(beg<end)    //  more than one element is in the list
     {
       P=Partition(A,beg,end)      // Gets the position of Pivot
       QuickSort(A,beg,P-1)        // Recursive call for Left side
       QuickSort(A,P+1,end)    // Recursive call for right side
     }

}

Partition(A,beg ,end)
{
    Pivot = a[beg],  i = low + 1,  j = end
  while (1)
  {
  while (i < end && Pivot > A[i])
    i++;
```

```
      [End While]

  while (Pivot < A[j])
  j--;
      [End While]

    if (i < j)
        Swap  A[i] and A[j]
    else
          {
          Swap  A[beg] and A[j]
          return j;
           }
  }
}
```

Complexity Analysis of Quick Sort:

Time Complexity:

* Best Case: $\Omega(Nlog(N))$
  The best-case scenario for quicksort occur when the pivot chosen at the each step divides the array into roughly equal halves. In this case, the algorithm will make balanced partitions, leading to efficient Sorting.
* Average Case:$\Theta(Nlog(N))$
  Quicksort's average-case performance is usually very good in practice, making it one of the fastest sorting Algorithm.
* Worst Case: $O(N^2)$
  The worst-case Scenario for Quicksort occur when the pivot at each step consistently results in highly unbalanced partitions. When the array is already sorted and the pivot is always chosen as the smallest or largest element. To mitigate the worst-case Scenario, various techniques are used such as choosing a good pivot (e.g., median of three) and using Randomized algorithm (Randomized Quicksort) to shuffle the element before sorting.

Space Complexity : O(1)
If we don't consider the recursive stack space. If we consider the recursive stack space then, in the worst case quicksort could make O(N).

Advantages of Quick Sort:

- It is a divide-and-conquer algorithm that makes it easier to solve problems.
- It is efficient on large data sets.

- It has a low overhead, as it only requires a small amount of memory to function.

Disadvantages of Quick Sort:

- It has a worst-case time complexity of $O(N^2)$, which occurs when the pivot is chosen poorly.
- It is not a good choice for small data sets.
- It is not a stable sort, meaning that if two elements have the same key, their relative order will not be preserved in the sorted output in case of quick sort, because here we are swapping elements according to the pivot's position (without considering their original positions).

5.1.6 Heap Sort

Heap sort processes the elements by creating the min-heap or max-heap using the elements of the given array. Min-heap or max-heap represents the ordering of array in which the root element represents the minimum or maximum element of the array.

Heap sort basically recursively performs two main operations -

- Build a heap H, using the elements of array.
- Repeatedly delete the root element of the heap formed in 1st phase.

What is a heap?

A heap is a complete binary tree, and the binary tree is a tree in which the node can have the utmost two children. A complete binary tree is a binary tree in which all the levels except the last level, i.e., leaf node, should be completely filled, and all the nodes should be left-justified.

There are two types of heaps:

1. Max Heap
2. Min Heap

Max Heap Property

1. $A[Parent(i)] \geq A[i]$, for all node i, except the root node
2. The value of the node is at most the value of its parent
3. Root stores the largest element of the tree
   Heap tree satisfies the max heap property is termed as Max heap

Min Heap

1. A[Parent(i)]≤A[i], for all node i, except the root node
2. Here the root node of a sub tree stores the smallest value compared to all other nodes in that subtree.
3. We can say that Root node stores the smallest element of the tree
   Heap tree satisfies the min heap property is termed as Min heap

What is heap sort?

Heapsort is a popular and efficient sorting algorithm. The concept of heap sort is to eliminate the elements one by one from the heap part of the list, and then insert them into the sorted part of the list.

Heapsort is the in-place sorting algorithm.

Heap Sort - Example Let's take an unsorted array and try to sort it using heap sort.

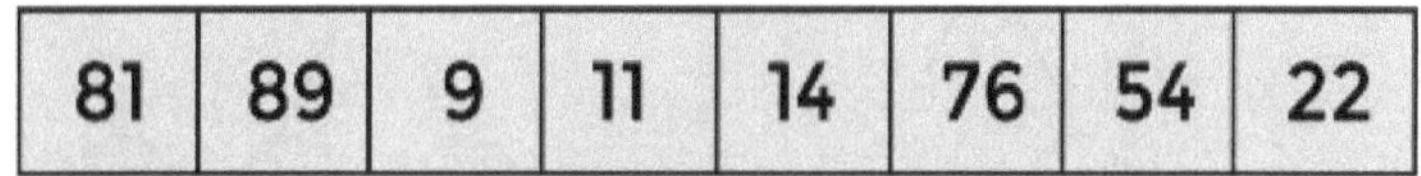

Figure 5.8: Unsorted Array

First, we have to construct a heap from the given array and convert it into max heap.

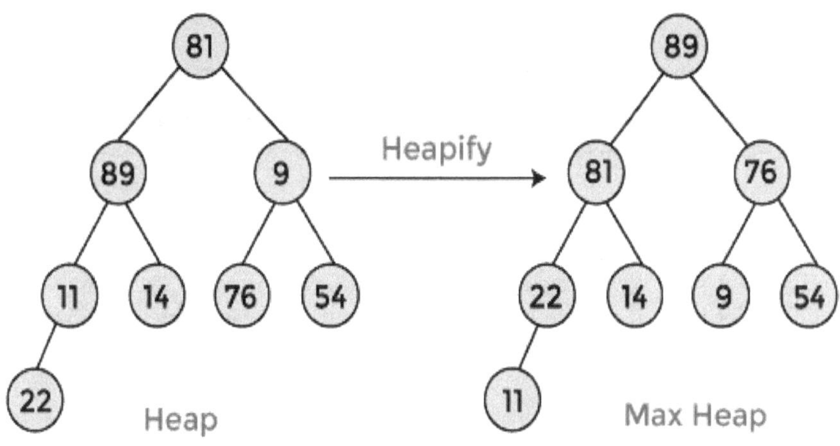

Figure 5.9: (i) Heap Tree (ii) Max Heap

After converting the given heap into max heap, the array elements are -

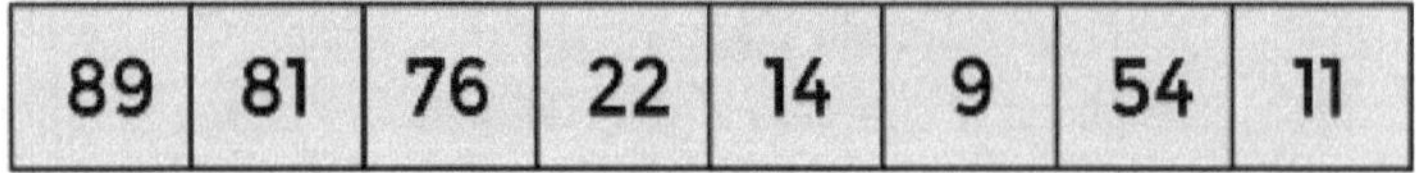

Figure 5.10: Array Representation of Max heap

Next, we have to delete the root element (89) from the max heap. To delete this node, we have to swap it with the last node, i.e. (11). After deleting the root element, we again have to heapify it to convert it into max heap.

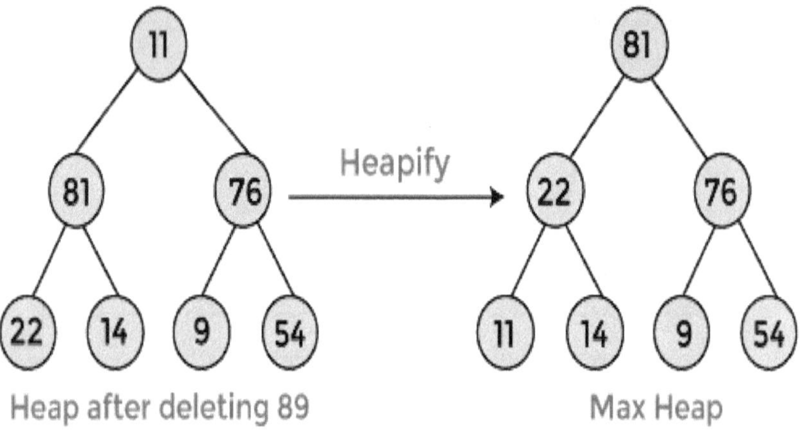

After swapping the array element 89 with 11, and converting the heap into max-heap, the elements of array are -

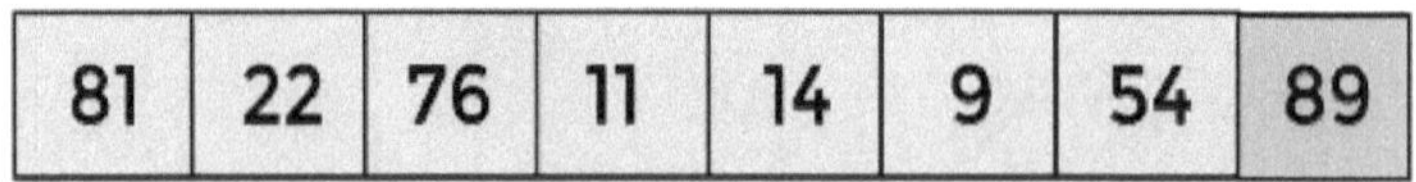

Figure 5.11: Max heap with last element sorted

In the next step, again, we have to delete the root element (81) from the max heap. To delete this node, we have to swap it with the last node, i.e. (54). After deleting the root element, we again have to heapify it to convert it into max heap.

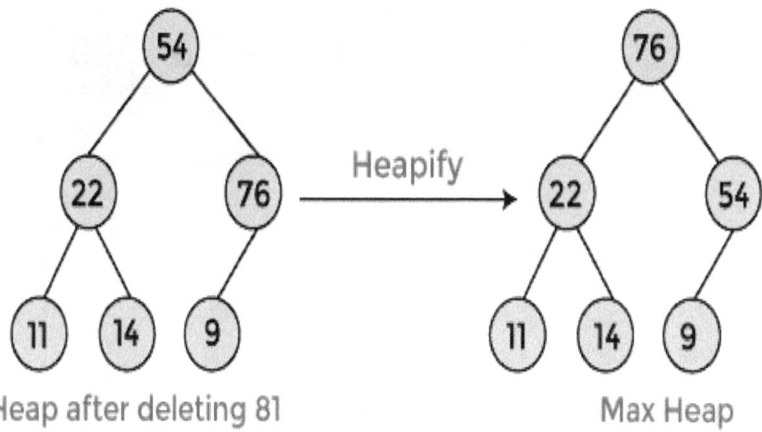

After swapping the array element 81 with 54 and converting the heap into max-heap, the elements of array are -

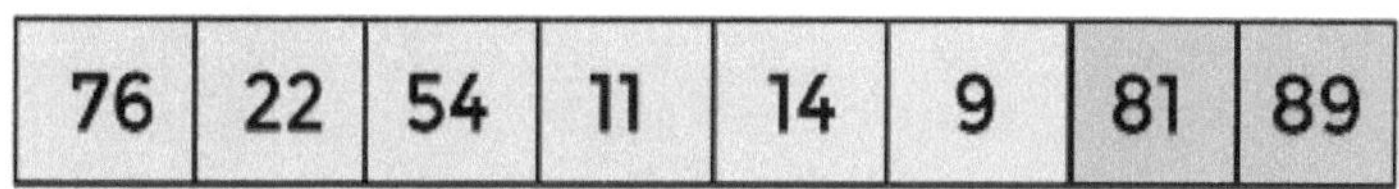

Figure 5.12: Max heap with last 2 elements sorted

In the next step, we have to delete the root element (76) from the max heap again. To delete this node, we have to swap it with the last node, i.e. (9). After deleting the root element, we again have to heapify it to convert it into max heap.

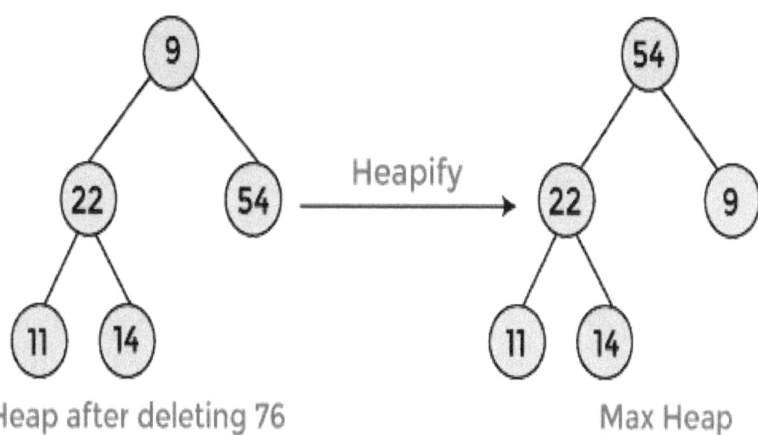

After swapping the array element 76 with 9 and converting the heap into max-heap, the elements of array are -

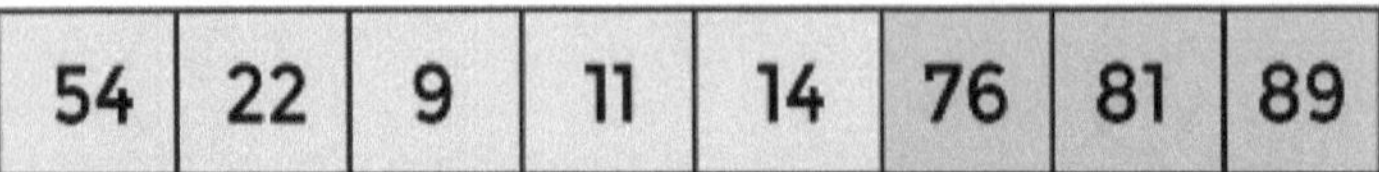

Figure 5.13: Max heap with last 3 elements sorted

In the next step, again we have to delete the root element (54) from the max heap. To delete this node, we have to swap it with the last node, i.e. (14). After deleting the root element, we again have to heapify it to convert it into max heap.

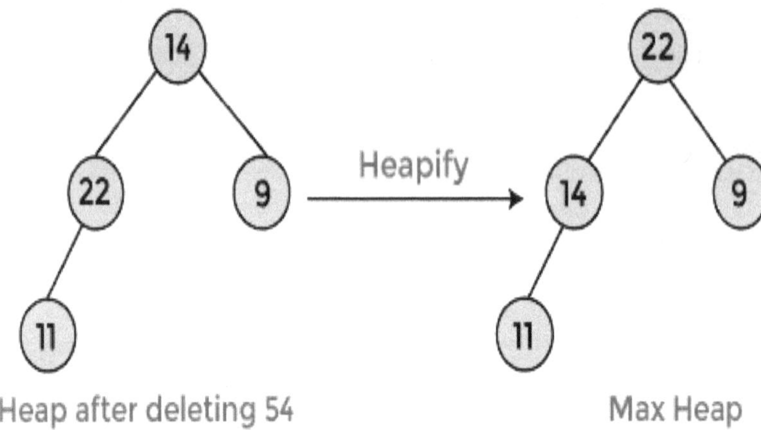

After swapping the array element 54 with 14 and converting the heap into max-heap, the elements of array are -

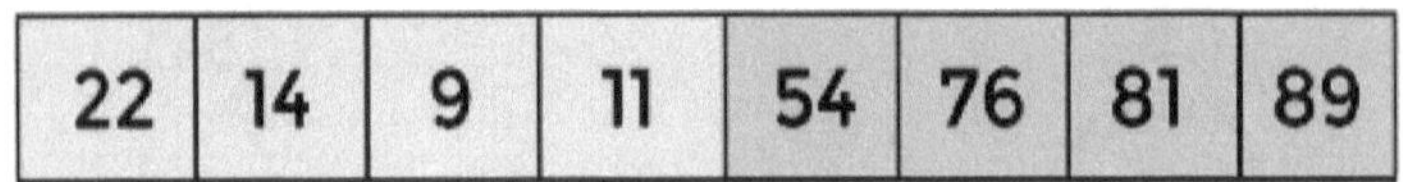

Figure 5.14: Max heap with last 4 elements sorted

In the next step, again we have to delete the root element (22) from the max heap. To delete this node, we have to swap it with the last node, i.e. (11). After deleting the root element, we again have to heapify it to convert it into max heap.

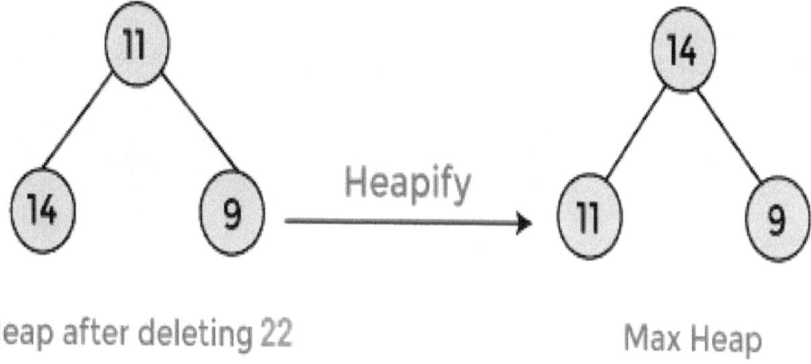

After swapping the array element 22 with 11 and converting the heap into max-heap, the elements of array are -

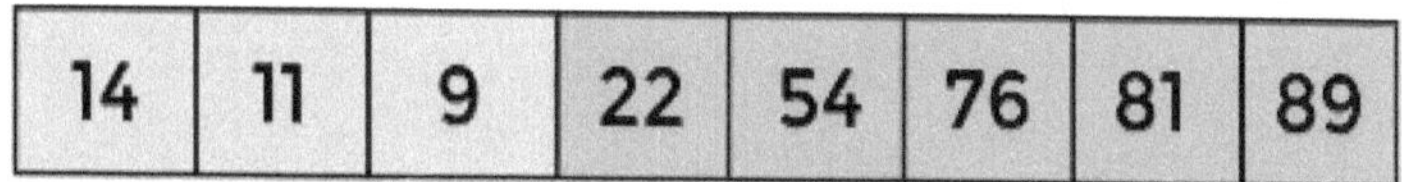

Figure 5.15: Max heap with last 5 elements sorted

In the next step, again we have to delete the root element (14) from the max heap. To delete this node, we have to swap it with the last node, i.e. (9). After deleting the root element, we again have to heapify it to convert it into max heap.

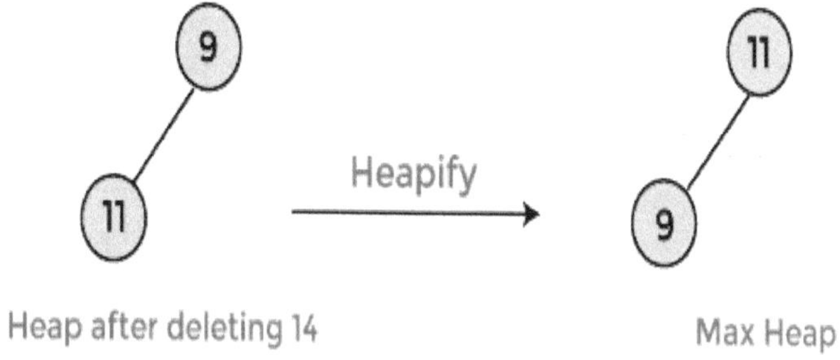

After swapping the array element 14 with 9 and converting the heap into max-heap, the elements of array are -

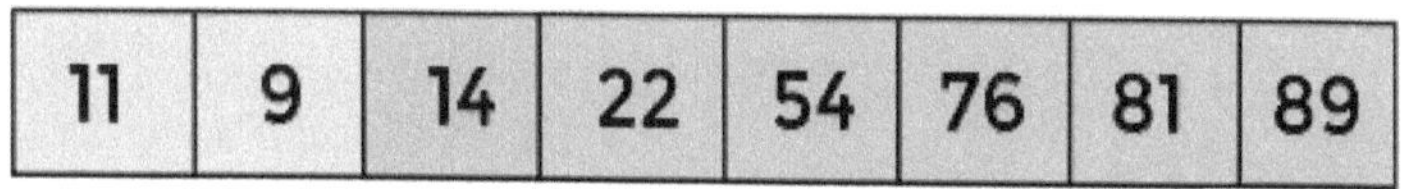

Figure 5.16: Max heap with last 6 elements sorted

In the next step, again we have to delete the root element (11) from the max heap. To delete this node, we have to swap it with the last node, i.e. (9). After deleting the root element, we again have to heapify it to convert it into max heap.

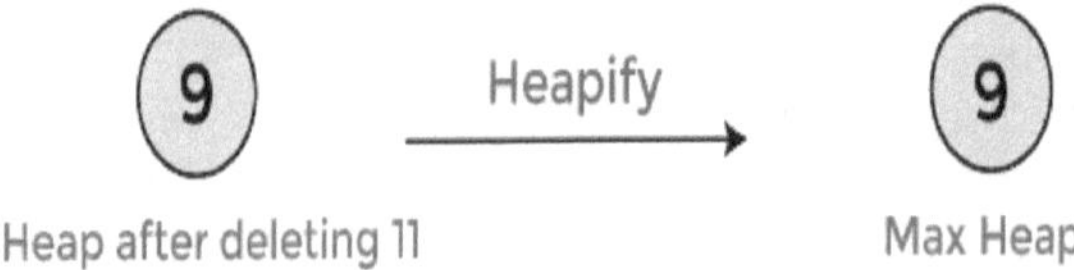

After swapping the array element 11 with 9, the elements of array are -

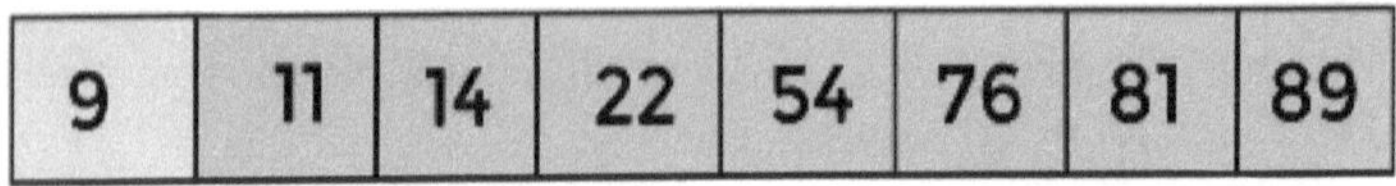

Figure 5.17: Max heap with last 7 elements sorted

Now, heap has only one element left. After deleting it, heap will be empty.

After completion of sorting, the array elements are -

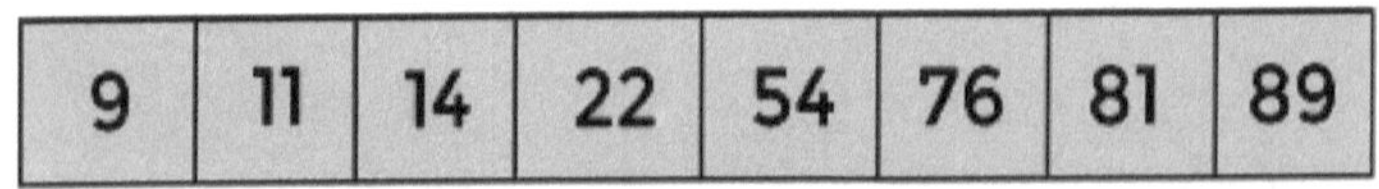

Figure 5.18: Sorted Array List

Now, the array is completely sorted.

Heap sort - Pseudocode

```
Algorithm: HeapSort(a,n)
{
    Heapify(a,n)                // Create a Max heap
    Size = n
    for i = n to 2 do
      { t = a[i]
        a[i] = a[1]     // Swap Root with Last element
```

```
            a[1] = t
            Size = Size - 1
            Adjust (a,1,Size)        // Rebuild the heap
        }
}

Algorithm: Heapify(a,n)
 {
    For ( i = n/2 ; i>=1 ; i--) do
        Adjust (a,i,n)


 }



Algorithm: Adjust(a,i,n)
{
j = 2*i,    item = a[i]
while( j <= n) do
  {
     if( j < n) and ( a[ j ] < a[ j+1 ]  )
             // compares left and right child
         j = j + 1   // larger number in jth position

    if( item >=a[ j ] ) then    // position for item found
      break               // Go to step 4

      a[ j/2 ] = a[ j ]
        j = 2*j
  }
a[ j/2 ] = item
}
```

Complexity Analysis of Heap Sort:

Time Complexity: $O(NlogN)$

Space Complexity : $O(1)$
Auxiliary Space: $O(\log n)$, due to the recursive call stack. However, auxiliary space can be $O(1)$ for iterative implementation.

Advantages of Heap Sort:

- Efficient Time Complexity: Heap Sort has a time complexity of $O(n \log n)$ in all cases. This makes it efficient for sorting large datasets. The log n factor comes from the height of the binary heap, and it ensures that the algorithm maintains good performance even with a large number of elements.

- Memory Usage – Memory usage can be minimal because apart from what is necessary to hold the initial list of items to be sorted, it needs no additional memory space to work.

- Simplicity – It is simpler to understand than other equally efficient sorting algorithms because it does not use advanced computer science concepts such as recursion.

Disadvantages of Quick Sort:

- Costly: Heap sort is costly.

- Unstable: Heap sort is unstable. It might rearrange the relative order.

- Efficient: Heap Sort is not very efficient when working with highly complex data.

Stability of Sorting Algorithms

An algorithm is said to be stable if the original order of elements having the same key is preserved even after sorting. For example, if the two elements of an array, arr[i] and arr[j], have the same key and i¡j, then after sorting, arr[i] should come before arr[j]. Algorithms like merge sort and insertion sort are known as stable sorting algorithms, whereas quick sort and heap sort are unstable sorting algorithms.

5.2 Hashing

Hashing is a technique or process of mapping keys, and values into the hash table by using a hash function. It is done for faster access to elements with a constant search time. The time complexity for searching using hashing is O(1). The efficiency of mapping depends on the efficiency of the hash function used.

The hash function maps the key into corresponding index of the array(hash table). The main idea behind any hashing technique is to find one-to-one correspondence between a key value and an index in the hash table where the key value can be placed.

Mathematically, this can be expressed as shown in figure below where K denotes a set of key values, I denote a range of indices, and H denotes the mapping function from K to I.

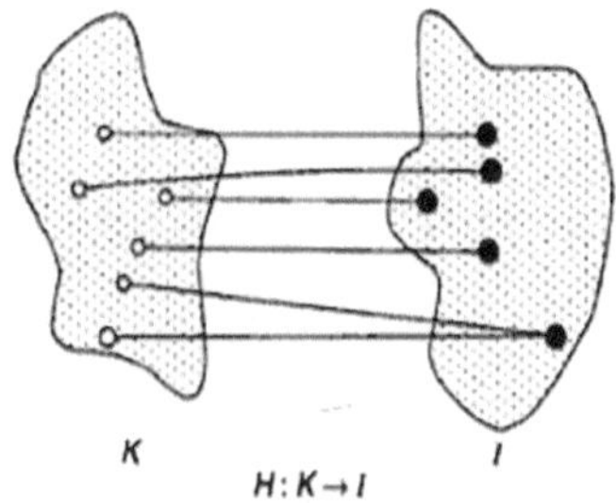

Figure 5.19: Mapping function from K to I

All key values are mapped into some indices and more than one key value may be mapped into an index value. The function that governs this mapping is called the hash function. There are two principal criteria in deciding hash function H:K-¿I as follows.

1. The function H should be very easy and quick to compute

2. It should be easy to implement

Example 1:
Consider a hash table of size 10 whose indices are 0,1,2,...9. Suppose a set of key values are 10,19,35,43,62,59,31,49,77,33. Consider the Hash function H(k) as to add the two digits in the key and take the digit at the unit place of the result as index , ignore the digits at tenth place if any.

K	I
10	1
19	0
35	8
43	7
62	8
59	4
31	4
49	3
77	4
33	6

$H: K \rightarrow I$

0	19
1	10
2	
3	49
4	59, 31, 77
5	
6	33
7	43
8	35, 62
9	

Hash table

5.2.1 Hash Functions

A hash function is a type of mathematical operation that takes an input (or key) and outputs a fixed-size result known as a hash code or hash value. The hash function must always yield the same hash code for the same input in order to be deterministic. Additionally, the hash function should produce a unique hash code for each input, which is known as the hash property.

There are different types of hash functions, including:

1. Division method

    Division method is one of the fast-hashing functions, and perhaps the most widely accepted. Here we choose a number h larger than the number n of keys in K. The hash function H(k) is then defined by

    H(k)=k MOD h if indices start from 0

    H(k)=[k MOD h] +1 if indices start from 1

    Where $k \in K$, a key value. And h is generally chosen to be a prime number and equal to the size of the hash table.
    The operator MOD defines the modulo operator, which gives the reminder when dividing k by h.

For example, if k=31 and h=13 then,

$$H(31)=31 \text{ MOD } 13=5 \text{ if indices start from } 0$$

$$H(31)=(31 \text{ MOD } 13)+1=6 \text{ if indices start from } 1$$

2. Mid Square Method

Another hash function which has been widely used in many applications is the mid square method. The hash function H is defined by H(k)=x, where x is obtained by selecting an appropriate number of bits or digits from the middle of the square of the key value k. For a three digit index requirement, after finding the square of key values, the digits at 2nd, 4th and 6th position are chosen as their hash values from right side.

For example-

k	:	1234	2345	3456
k^2	:	1522756	5499025	11943936
H(k)	:	525	492	933

Figure 5.20: Mid Square Method examples

Here, 3 examples are shown. For key 1234, k^2 is 1522756, extract 2nd, 4th and 6th digits from right, to get the value as 525.

3. Folding Method

Here k is partitioned into a number of parts k1 , k2....kn where each part has equal number of digits as the required address(index) width. Then these parts are added together in the hash function.
H(k)=k1+k2+...+kn, where the last carry, if any is ignored.

There are mainly three variations of this method.

  (a) Pure folding method
  (b) Fold shifting method
  (c) Fold boundary method

Key values k :	1522756	5499025	11943936
Chopping :	01 52 27 56	05 49 90 25	11 94 39 36
Pure folding :	01+52+27+56=136	05+49+90+25=169	11+94+39+36=180
Fold Shifting:	10+52+72+56=190	50+49+09+25=133	11+94+93+36=234
Fold Boundary	10+52+27+65=154	50+49+90+52=241	11+94+39+63=207

Figure 5.21: Folding Method examples

4. Digit Analysis Method

This method is particularly useful in the case of static files where the key values of all the records are known in advance. The basic idea of this hash function is to form hash address by extracting or shifting the extracted digits of the key. For any given set of keys, the position in the keys and the same rearrangement pattern must be used consistently. The decision for extraction and rearrangement is finalized after analysis of hash functions under different criteria.

Example:
Given a key value 6732541, it can be transformed to the hash address 427 by extracting the digits from even position. And then reversing this combination.ie 724 is the hash address.

5.2.2 Collision Resolution/Overflow Handling Techniques

In hashing, we use the hash function is used to find the index of the array for a given key. The hash function may return the same hash value for two or more keys. When two or more keys have the same hash value, a collision happens. To handle this collision, we use collision resolution techniques.

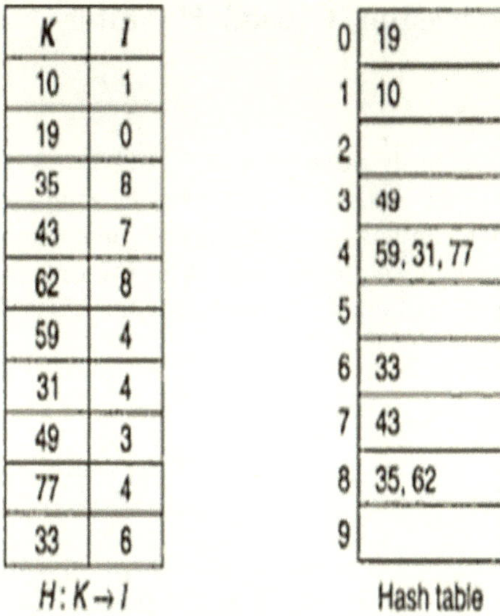

The figure above shows , there are more than one value being mapped at location 4 and 8. This is called collision.

There are several methods to resolve collision. Two important methods are listed below:

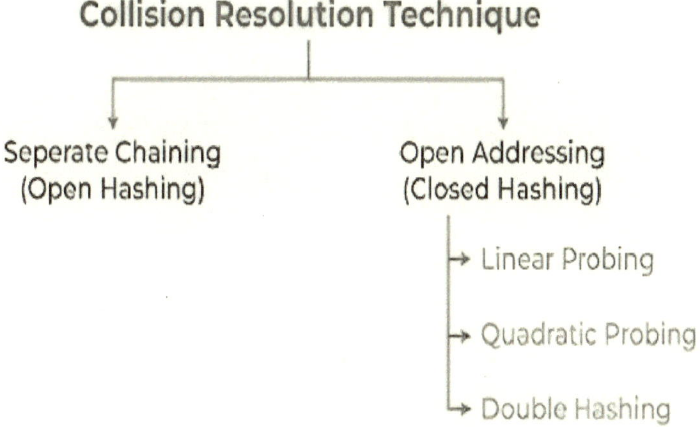

Figure 5.22: Classification of Collision Resolution Techniques

5.2.3 Open Addressing/Closed Hashing

1. Linear Probing

Suppose there is a hash table of size h and the key value is mapped to location i, with a hash function. The closed hashing can then be stated as follows. Start with the hash address where the collision has occurred, let it be i. Then carry out a sequential search in the order:- i, i+1, i+2... h, 1, 2 ..., i-1. The search will continue until any one of the following occurs

- The key value is found

- An unoccupied location is found

- The searches reaches the location where search had started.

The first case corresponds to successful search, and the other two case corresponds to unsuccessful search. Here the hash table is considered circular, so that when the last location is reached, the search proceeds to the first location of the table. This is why the technique is termed closed hashing. Since the technique searches in a straight line, it is alternatively termed as linear probing.

Example- Assume there is a hash table of size 10 and hash function uses the division method of remainder modulo 7, namely H(k)=k(MOD 7)+1.The construction of hash table for the key values 15,11,25,16,9,8,12 is illustrated below.

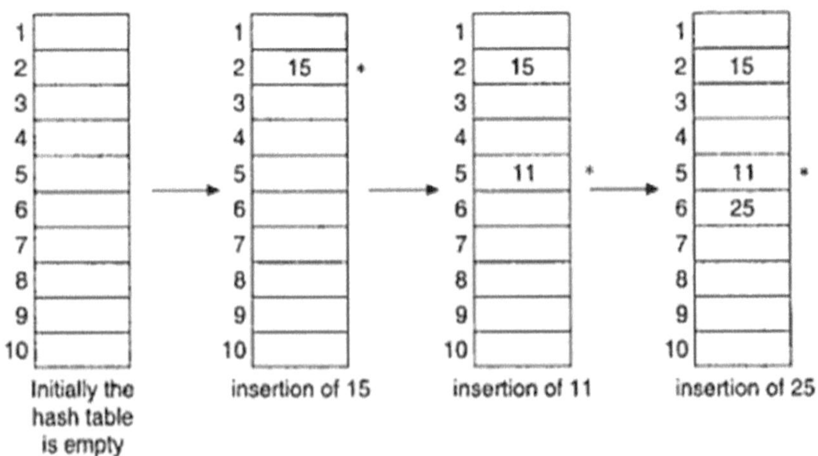

Figure 5.23: Key values entered in order 15,11,25

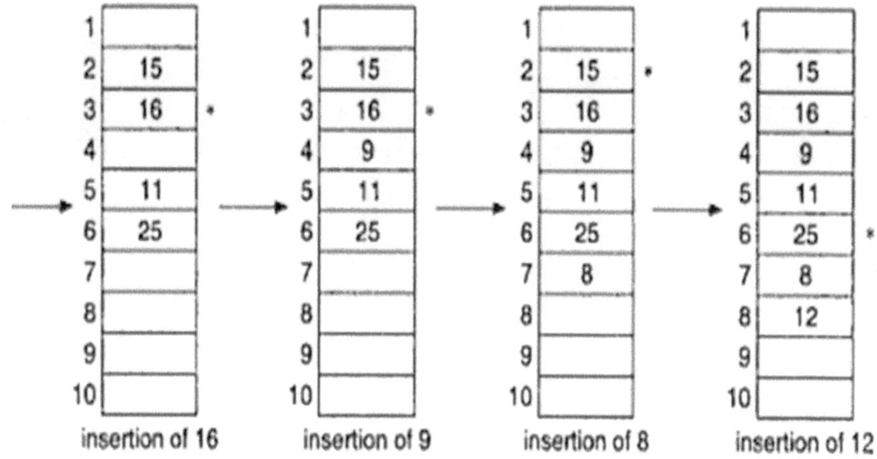

Figure 5.24: Key values entered in order 16,9,8,12

Drawback of Linear Probing

The major drawback of closed hashing is that as half of the hash table is filled, there is a tendency towards clustering. That is key values are clustered in large groups and as a result sequential search becomes slower and slower. This kind of clustering is known as **primary clustering**.

The following are some solutions to avoid this situation are Quadratic probing Random probing and Double hashing

2. Quadratic Probing

It is a collision resolution method that eliminates the primary clustering problem of linear probing. For linear probing, if there is a collision at location i, then the next locations i+1, i+2..etc are probed. But in quadratic probing next locations to be probed are $i+1^2, i+2^2, i+3^2$ ..etc. This method substantially reduces primary clustering, but it doesn't probe all the locations in the table.

3. Random Probing

Instead of using linear probing that generates sequential locations in order, a random location is generated using random probing. An example of pseudo random number generator that generates such a random sequence is given below:

$$I = (i + m)MODh + 1$$

Where m and h are prime numbers.

For example, if m=5, and h=11 and initially i=2 then random probing generates the random sequence

$$I=(2+5)\text{MOD } 11 + 1 \qquad I = 8$$

Next value is calculated as

$$I = (8+5)\text{MOD } 11 + 1 \qquad I = 3$$

And rest generates the sequence 8,3,9,4,10,5,11,6,1,7,2

Here all numbers are generated between 1 and 11 in a random order. Primary clustering problem is solved. Whereas there is an issue of clustering when two keys are hashed into the same location and then they make use of the same sequence locations generated by the random probing, which is called as **secondary clustering**.

4. Double Hashing

An alternative approach to solve the problem of secondary clustering is to make use of second hash function in addition to the first one.

Double hashing has the ability to have a low collision rate, as it uses two hash functions to compute the hash value and the step size. This means that the probability of a collision occurring is lower than in other collision resolution techniques such as linear probing or quadratic probing.

double hashing is defined as

$$H(k,i) = [H1(k) + i * H2(k)] \text{ MOD TABLE \_SIZE}$$

H1(k) is initially used hash function and H2(k) is the second one. These two functions are defined as

$$H1(k)=(k \text{ MOD } h1) \text{ and } H2(k)=(k \text{ MOD } (h2))$$

The use of secondary hash function H2(k) after the collision, helps us to reach new locations on the hash table. Each new location is at a distance of 1*H2(k), 2*H2(k), 3*H2(k).....as i =1,2,3...

This results in a non-linear fashion of addressing hash-table which reduces the number of collisions. A very important point to be considered is that both the hash functions should be computed in order of O(1) time.

Example:

Suppose, we have a hash table of size 11. We want to insert keys 20,34,45,75,

61,69 in the hash table. Let's insert the keys into hash table using the following double hash functions:

h1(k) = k mod 11   (first hash function)

h2(k) = k mod 7   (second hash function)

$$H(k,i) = [H1(k) + i * H2(k)] \text{ MOD TABLE\_SIZE}$$

$$H(k,i) = [k \bmod 11 + i * k \bmod 7] \text{ MOD } 11$$

First, we will create a empty hash table of size 11.

Steps	Key	Hash Function	Index	Description
1	20	H(20) = 20 mod 11	9	No collision occurs.
2	34	H(34) = 34 mod 11	1	No collision occurs.
3	45	H(45) = 45 mod 11	1	Collision occur because index 1 is already occupied by 34. Now we will use the second hash function to calculate the index for the key 45
		H(45,1) =[45 mod 11+ (1*(45 mod 7)]%11]	4	Here, we have taken the value if i 1 because first collision occurs.
4	75	H(75) = 75 mod 11	9	Collision occur because index 9 is already occupied by 20. Now we will use the second hash function to calculate the index for the key 75 with i=1
		H(75,1) =[75 mod 11+ (1*(75 mod 7)]%11]	3	No collision occurs.
5	61	H(61) =61 mod 11	6	No collision occurs.

Figure 5.25: Hash values calculation for 20,34,45,75,61

6	69	$h_1(69)$ = 69 mod 11	3	Collision occur because index 3 is already occupied by 75. Now we will use the second hash function to calculate the index for the key 69 with i=1.
		H(69,1) =[69 mod 11+ (1*(69 mod 7)]%11] = (3+(1*3))	6	Again, collision occur. The index 6 is already occupied by 61.
		H(69,2) =[69 mod 11+ (2*(69 mod 7)]%11] = (3+(2*3))	9	Collision occur because index 9 is already occupied by 20. Now we will use the second hash function to calculate the index for the key 69 with i=3
		H(69,3) =[69 mod 11+ (3*(69 mod 7)]%11] = (3+(3*3))	1	Collision occur because index 1 is already occupied by 34. Now we will use the second hash function to calculate the index for the key 69 with i=4.
		H(69,4) =[69 mod 11+ (4*(69 mod 7)]%11] = (3+(4*3))	4	Collision occur because index 4 is already occupied by 45. Now we will use the second hash function to calculate the index for the key 69 with i=5
		H(69,5) =[69 mod 11+ (5*(69 mod 7)]%11] = (3+(5*3))	7	No collision occurs.

Figure 5.26: Hash values calculation for 69

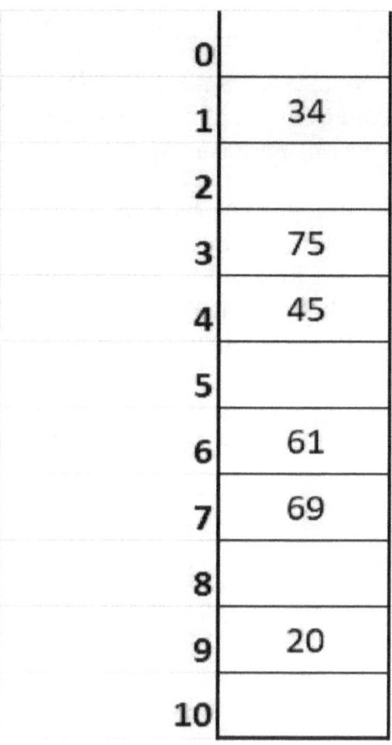

Figure 5.27: Key values entered in order 20,34,45,75,61,69

Advantages of Double hashing

- The advantage of Double hashing is that it is one of the best forms of probing, producing a uniform distribution of records throughout a hash table.

- This technique does not yield any clusters.

- It is one of the effective methods for resolving collisions.

Drawbacks of Double Hashing

First, it requires the use of two hash functions, which can increase the computational complexity of the insertion and search operations. Second, it requires a good choice of hash functions to achieve good performance. If the hash functions are not well-designed, the collision rate may still be high.

5.2.4   Open Hashing/ Chaining

Closed hashing method for collision resolution deals with arrays as hash tables and thus random positions can be quickly referred. Two main disadvantages of closed hashing are

- It is very difficult to handle the problem of overflow in a satisfactory manner

- The key values are haphazardly intermixed and, on the average majority of the key values are from their hash locations increasing the number of probes which degrades the overall performance.

To resolve these problems another hashing method called open hashing or separate chaining is used. The chaining method uses hash table as an array of pointers. Each pointer points a linked list. That is here the hash table is an array of list of headers. Illustrated below is an example with hash table of size10 for key values 24,12,10,64,36,57,43,19,16,39,54,82.

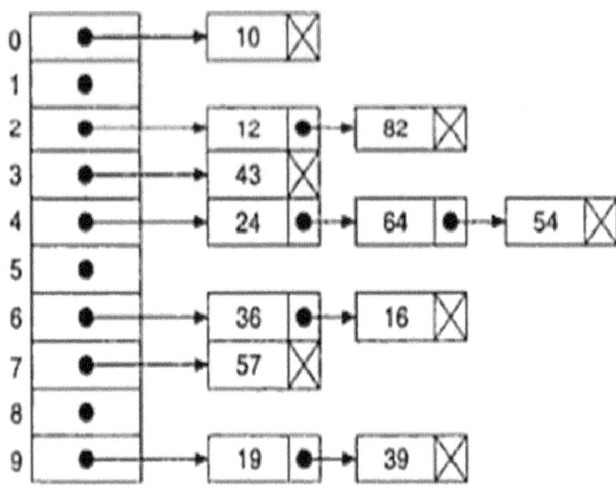

Figure 5.28: Hash values calculation for 24,12,10,64,36,57,43,19,16,39,54,82